BIG BUTTS, FAT THIGHS, AND OTHER SECRETS TO SUCCESS

BIG BUTTS, FAT THIGHS, AND OTHER SECRETS TO SUCCESS

Empowering Women to Be Real in Business and in Life

LAURA BLACK

Cazco Press
LCB Ventures, LLC
Baltimore, MD

AUTHOR'S DISCLAIMER: In many instances, the names and identifying
characteristics of people mentioned in this book have been changed to protect
the privacy of those involved. In some cases a single character is a combination of
several real people. Additionally, some events or people have been magnified or
altered to more fully illustrate a point.

This publication contains only the opinions and ideas of its author. It is sold
with the understanding that the author is not rendering professional advice or
services. The ideas, procedures, exercises, suggestions and advice contained
in this book are not intended as a substitute for consulting with appropriate
professionals. The author will not be liable or responsible for any loss, damage or
claim allegedly arising from any information, opinions, exercises or suggestions
contained in this book.

First Edition

10 9 8 7 6 5 4 3 2 1

Design by Sensical Design & Communication, Washington, DC

PRINTED IN THE UNITED STATES OF AMERICA

To my children and grandchildren—
Danny, Laura, Andy, Kristin, Jackie, Addie, Connor, and Zachary—Never allow anything, especially yourself, to block your path.

To Charles—
You've always accepted my big butts with unwavering love and compassion.

To Mom and Dad—
You showed me that I control my destiny.

CONTENTS

INTRODUCTION

I REALLY WANTED THIS ACCOUNT. BUSINESS FROM THIS FORTUNE 500 company could have a significant impact on my own business. In preparation for my presentation, I researched and reviewed everything I could find about the company. On the plane to their corporate headquarters, I studied some more. Before I knew it, I was standing in the lobby of a towering building. I gave the security guard the necessary information, allowing me access to the executive floor. My heart was pounding. In just a moment, I would meet the decision maker in her office, before continuing to lunch in the private dining room where I would make my pitch.

Her assistant ushered me to the executive suite. I straightened my back, put a smile on my face and held out my hand for our introduction. After exchanging the normal pleasantries, I glanced toward her desk. On the corner, I spied a Weight Watchers point counter. "You do points?" I enthusiastically questioned. "Yes, I've been counting points for several months," she replied. "So do I!" I shared, relief spreading through me. We enjoyed a low-point lunch. We talked about diets, calories, and the challenges of weight loss. Of course, we also discussed business and why my company would best fulfill her needs. I got the account.

Now, more than ever, whether you aspire to become the CEO of a Fortune 500 company, a top salesperson in your organization, an effective fund-raiser for your child's school, or find employment in a challenging economy, you must develop the strong networking and rainmaking skills necessary to build key, influential relationships.

As women, it is easy and natural to connect to one another by sharing our "vulnerabilities." Seated at our kitchen tables or sipping Cosmos at our favorite restaurant, we do not hesitate to bond with other women over our weight being too high, or the availability of eligible men being too low. Yet, once we enter our place of work, or a fund-raising committee meeting, a force seems to descend upon us. We become "Stepford" women. The same vulnerabilities that we share freely over coffee, we consider fatal if even mentioned in work like situations. Consequently, we spend eight hours a day, five days a week, trying to hide our real selves and covering up our big butts; playing our ill-conceived role of business woman as dictated to us by well-meaning mentors or glossy business magazines.

Before I was even old enough to enter the workforce, trying to hide my big butt was my life's mission. For way too many years, I was consumed with shame over my fat body—my big butt and fat thighs. Shallow measurements of self-worth were especially rigid for me, growing up in South Florida. I believed that my pudgy physique rendered me powerless and insignificant. By using the principles set forth in this book, I was able to transform myself from a fat girl apologizing for her very existence, to an existence defined by business and leadership success.

How ironic, the very big butt that defined my being was, in the end, what allowed me to form the relationships necessary to reach the highest levels of success. By accepting my own big butt and allowing others to see it; I was implicitly giving others permission to share their own vulnerabilities. I was sending them the message that they did not have to try to be perfect around me. They were grateful that in my presence, they could reveal their real selves and form connections based on truth, rather than pretense. They did not have to work at keeping up a wall of defenses. They did not have to meet some superficial expectation to receive validation from me. As a result, they liked me and wanted to see me succeed. My phone calls were returned. I was given a chance at their business. They were willing to introduce me to other decision makers. They tried to help me in nonprofit endeavors. They agreed to be part of my committees. I was real. They knew I liked them and would not judge them. I allowed them to be themselves—big butts and all.

Throughout this journey, I have had the privilege of working with thousands of women in a multitude of venues. I have hired, supervised, mentored, and counseled women in all stages of their careers. I have taught women rainmaking skills for business and fund-raising skills for nonprofits. I have motivated individuals to reach their personal goals and rallied groups to reach community goals. From working with this wide array of women, I have come to realize that everyone has a big butt.

For some, our big butt is literal. It may be so big that we have given up trying to squeeze it into the latest designer jeans. Or, we may have those fat thighs that come complete with cottage-cheese looking dimples. Maybe we have breasts that sag all the way down to our waist, hair that is totally unmanageable, or a large protruding nose.

For others, our big butt is figurative. It may be our fear that we are a failure because our position was eliminated. Or, our guilt for leaving our children while we are at work. For many, it is that voice, whispering in our ear, saying that we are just not good enough. Our big butt may be our mistaken belief that we must be perfect. Our big butt is whatever insecurity, whatever imperfection, is keeping us from reaching our goals. The size of our butt usually has nothing to do with reality and everything to do with perception.

We can spend a lifetime and life savings trying to rid ourselves of our big butts. We can try to camouflage them with clothing or hide them with cosmetic surgery. If it is an intangible, such as our fear of failure, we either pretend it is not there; or alternatively, we overcompensate for the fact that it is. Yet, even if we manage to diminish its size or get rid of it, it seems to always exist in our minds. Unfortunately, the harder we try to escape from it, the larger it seems to appear.

While we desperately try to hide them, our imperfections, with a voice of their own, speak volumes. They may cause us to walk into a job interview looking downward, trying to shrink from scrutiny. Or, they may urge us to hedge our opinions and doubt our conclusions when sitting around the boardroom table. In short, we enter the workplace, mistakenly convinced that we cannot be ourselves and must hide our imperfections at all costs. As a result, we forgo our natural way of communication. By protecting our big butt and hiding our true self, not only do we discourage relationship building, but we actually push people away and sabotage our own success in forging critical business connections.

I do not want you to waste another minute of your life focusing on your big butt or other imperfections. Instead, I want you to embrace your vulnerabilities and go on to conquer your dreams.

Big Butts, Fat Thighs, and Other Secrets to Success will not tell you how to get rid of your big butt. Unlike all the books that crowd your shelves, this is not a weight-loss book. There will be no diet tricks or low-calorie recipes. Likewise, this is not like the other business books out there, pushing you to act like someone other than yourself in order to achieve success.

Big Butts, Fat Thighs, and Other Secrets to Success will set forth specific steps for you to follow to accept your imperfections and refocus your identity. In so doing, you will acquire the confidence and competence to build the network of genuine relationships that are vital for your success. Here at last is a book that teaches you how to win just by being yourself—big butt, fat thighs and all!

Part I

DON'T LET YOUR BIG BUTT BE YOUR BIG *BUT*

IN THE FOLLOWING CHAPTERS I WILL TAKE YOU THROUGH THE steps that will enable you to move forward and escape from the confines of your big butt. You will learn, as I did, to accept your imperfections and realize they are merely a part of you— they do not define you. Ultimately, you will learn to stop allowing your big butt to keep you from reaching your goals: to stop it from being your big *but*.

Chapter One describes the anguish of growing up as a fat child in a culture that idolizes thinness and beauty. Chapter Two shows you how to identify your big butt. Whether it is a physical attribute or an emotional impediment, you must become aware of how your big butt is blocking your path to success. In Chapter Three, you will continue on your journey by delving into the full spectrum of unintended consequences that may arise when you carry around the weight of your big butt. In Chapter Four, we will make sure that you are ready to disempower your big butt and instead, empower yourself. Finally, your newfound awareness will help you through the process of acceptance in Chapter Five.

Chapter One

MY BIG BUTT BLOCKED THE SUN

I WAS A FAT GIRL GROWING UP IN ONE OF THE WORST PLACES IN the world for fat girls, Miami. It is the self-proclaimed capital of the magnificent body; defined by tight butts, firm thighs, and flat stomachs. It is the home of the beautiful people, a haven for models and movie stars. Their buff and perfected physiques are typically complemented with smooth, clear complexions and long, straight, usually blonde hair.

It seemed that wherever I turned, I was surrounded by these stunning women in their short shorts and jogging bras effortlessly running, biking, skating, swimming, boating, or playing tennis or golf. I could not escape them. When they were not exercising, they could be found stretched out on reclining chairs or towels, wearing those microscopic bikinis, offering their perfectly toned bodies for all to admire.

Of course, their bodies were adorned with only the "right" clothing and accessories. To this end, they spent an exorbitant amount of time and money trying to access the perfect combination of garments and garnishes that best accentuated their extraordinary figures. All attire had to carry the proper brand names. Only the very latest fashions would suffice.

I understood the rules, but was unable to follow them. Unfortunately, the right designer names did not come in plus sizes. This added insult to injury. Not only was I fat, I could not even be fashionably fat. For me, shopping was a nightmare. I would have to sneak into fat girls stores and pray that no one I knew saw me. My goal could not be fashion; I was happy to settle for garments that would camouflage my big butt and fat thighs. I remember my frustrated mother and me shopping for my junior-high-school wardrobe. After looking through too many stores, we finally hit upon a dress that fit me. It was an empire waist that came in several hideous prints. We bought one of each design. These dresses might have received compliments at the yearly dance at an assisted living facility.

My extremely frizzy hair was another challenge. Of course, the beautiful girls also had beautiful hair. Looking back, a significant chunk of my childhood was dedicated to trying to tackle the hair issue. I figured that if I could at least have straight, beautiful hair, I might fit in. A fat, straight-haired girl might have a chance. A fat, frizzy-haired girl would not. To this end, I tried using huge hair curlers. When they didn't work, I resorted to jumbo, orange juice cans. First, I would pull a small section of my hair as straight as possible, stretching it tightly around the can. I continued this process, section by section, until I could no longer fit any additional cans on my head. I anchored the hair with bobby pins. I would lie down at night with these huge cans in my hair, desperately trying to find a comfortable position for sleep.

In the morning I awoke to a sore neck from a night of various acrobatic sleeping positions. I would stand in front of my dresser mirror, anxiously removing one curler at a time, and rejoicing in the appearance of my semi straight hair. But, as soon as I walked outside, the straight hair facade was over. It was a useless battle: my newly straight hair versus the Miami humidity. The humidity always won. It took only moments until the frizz returned with a vengeance.

I ached to be accepted. I pined for friends. I felt totally alone in the world. The beautiful girls would only be seen with other beautiful girls. The boys would only be seen with the beautiful girls. Even other non-beautiful people did not want to be seen with me, as if their mere association would accentuate their own imperfections.

My parents eventually decided to try a different tack and increase my physical activity. The first attempt was baton lessons. Once a week, I took my baton and tried to learn different twirling techniques. My greatest memory from this endeavor, however, was not the baton twirling itself, but the entrepreneurial opportunity it afforded me. I would come home from my baton lesson, round up the neighborhood girls, and charge them for my makeshift classes. I never became physically fit. I did not lose any weight. But, I did earn some money.

From there we moved to numerous other physical endeavors. Perhaps the most ridiculous was ballet lessons. I tried so hard. "Come on girls, let's get in position one," the instructor cajoled. My wide feet and fat thighs just didn't belong in those ridiculous stances. It was the most unnatural thing I ever experienced. I would go home, holding on to a makeshift bar, and try to emulate the ludicrous positions. No amount of practice could give me a sense of flexibility, grace, or coordination. My short career imploded when I graduated to toe shoes.

I was so proud the day I was finally able to elevate and balance my fat body onto the tiny metal tips of those outlandish contraptions. Holding my breath, I raised my head high, put a smile across my face, and reveled in the glory of beating the anatomical odds. Gliding across the studio floor, in line with my fellow ballerinas, I allowed my eyes to gaze across the room. I was secretly hoping to witness the admiration of our audience, which was made up of the parents of the other hopeful ballerinas.

"They're looking at me," I realized. Innocently, my sense of achievement heightened, as I thought they were impressed with my hard fought success. I held my head even higher, until I overheard the whispers, still echoing today, "How ridiculous. Look at that fat girl trying to stay up on her toes. She doesn't belong in this class!"

Aside from some of my early entrepreneurial activities, such as giving baton lessons, I spent way too much time alone, feeling depressed and generally miserable. My fragile veil of self-esteem continued to unravel, until, it disappeared. There seemed no end to the tortuous existence of being fat. "I" was my big butt. My identity began and ended there. My big butt and fat thighs blocked the sun, blocked the light, and blocked my hopes and dreams. It was time to make a change.

The process took not days, weeks or months, but years. It was not purposeful. There was not a book, a prescription, a single mentor, a single inspiration, a single solution. It was slow, often misguided. There were many missteps, many wrong turns, yet, eventually, I found my soul, my spirit, and myself.

My wisdom was hard won. But, now, decades later, I have the ability to articulate and share the process that freed me from the worship of artificial ideals; the process that gave me freedom, actualization, and success—that gave me life.

I am good enough. I know this now. I have successfully emerged from a destructive emotional journey. How I wish I could have saved my younger self from her anguished existence. How I wish I could have kept her from defining her worth by defunct criteria. How I wish I could have kept her from acting out in damaging ways based on her faulty conclusions. I desperately wish I could have saved her sooner.

The good news is that you do not have to wait a moment longer. You no longer need to be defined by your imperfections. In the following chapters I will show you how to successfully liberate yourself from the confines of your own big butt, wherever you happen to be in your life's journey.

Chapter Two

IDENTIFYING YOUR BIG BUTT

BEFORE WE CAN LEARN TO ACCEPT OUR BIG BUTTS, WE MUST clearly identify them. For me, this was easy. I had many big butts. From my frizzy curly hair, to my big butt and cellulite-ridden thighs, I despised my physical appearance. What is holding you back? What is the source of that tiny voice in your head whispering that you are not good enough, smart enough, attractive enough, prepared enough, fill-in- the-blank enough? What is keeping you from confidently moving forward with your life? What is your big butt? If you don't know or aren't sure, let's find out.

Find Your Space

Find a place that allows you to escape from your everyday worries, thoughts, and responsibilities, a place where you can clear your head and get in touch with your authentic self. Many people find their space through meditation, yoga, or other mindfulness exercises. Others find their space outdoors while bike riding or walking. They find that movement and the accompanying chemical changes encourage freedom and creativity. Some people have a favorite chair or a special corner in a cozy room. It really doesn't matter where your space is located in your physical surroundings and in your mind, as long as it is accessible and allows you uninterrupted contemplation.

Once you have your space, make sure you use it. As women, we too often put ourselves last, and do not or cannot allow ourselves the essential time to just be. Strive to spend time in your space at least four times a week. The longer you can spend, the better, but even ten minutes is better than nothing.

Once you are in your space, begin to focus on identifying your big butt by asking yourself the following questions:

- What part or parts of my body am I embarrassed about?

- What is it about me that I think is not good enough?

- What don't I like about my personality?

- What do I hate about myself?

- What aspect of myself do I try to hide from others?

- What is it about me that I apologize for?

- If I could change anything about myself, what would it be?

You might find your answers while physically in your space. Or, your time there may simply help you to clear your mind, allowing thoughts and revelations to come later, when some unforeseen stimulus may serve as the trigger that helps you to identify your big butt.

As your start this journey, new thoughts may spring forth anytime or in any place. It is essential that you record these insights while they are fresh. I suggest carrying a small note-book in your purse, or using a note application on your cell phone so that you can easily record your ideas. Once a week, look through all your notes. Themes will emerge. You will soon be able to identify what it is that is holding you back, your big butt.

I Could _____ If Only _____

Another simple tool to help with the identification process is filling in the blanks in the following sentence: "I could _____ if only _____." The first blank is your goals and dreams. The second is your big butt.

Maybe you want to manage a department or a firm. Per-haps you strive to become the CEO for the company you work for, or you have a great idea and want to start your own busi-ness. Possibly, you want to reinvent yourself and go back to school or move to another part of the world. These goals are the first blank.

The second blank, your big butt, is whatever is stopping you from achieving your goal. What is keeping you from mak-ing it happen? What is keeping you from getting out there networking and building powerful relationships?

Go to your space and ask yourself the question: I could _____, if only _____. In answering this question, it may be helpful to think about an opportunity you had, or an opportunity you could have created. What held you back? Fill in the blank. For example, I could mingle more at firm parties, *if only* I weren't overweight, and therefore not attractive. Or, I could have taken that promotion, *if only*, I were smarter. I could leave my boring job and look for something more exciting, *if only*, I could handle change.

The blank is your big butt — your big *but*. Realize how much power *you* have given it. You have allowed it to stop you from being who you really want to be. You have allowed it to identify you. Does it deserve that much power?

Tara has worked as a departmental supervisor for a manufacturing company for over 20 years. As far back as she can remember, she has been unhappy and dreads going to work each morning. "Sunday nights are awful," she sighs, "but what choice do I have? I have job security and benefits, how could I even think about leaving?" This is the story she tells herself. She has told herself this story for over 19 years. She has told the story for so long that it has become her reality. She believes her own fiction.

Tara does not realize that she has the power over her big butt. She is not allowing herself to take charge and find a more meaningful position. In fact, in the last six months, she's had at least one opportunity and let it pass. She was at a party where she met the owner of a small company involved in the distribution of a product very similar to that of her current employer. She could have easily talked to him to see if there were any openings at his company or if he could help her find employment within the industry. Instead, she did nothing.

Tara had grown up in a small, Mayberry-like southern town. She never had an opportunity to travel, and went to a community college close to home. Her current job was only 20 minutes from her childhood home. To expand her employment opportunities, she would have to venture out of her geographic comfort zone.

The problem is that Tara feels self-conscious and inferior about her lack of exposure to other, more sophisticated places. She sees herself as a small-town girl unable to fit in with the environment of a larger city. In her mind, she is safe where she is, but, if put into a new situation, her unsophistication, her big butt, would be revealed, and she would fail.

She filled in the blanks in the big butt exercise in this way: "I could leave my job and find one that is more fulfilling, *if only*, I was worldlier." Tara had successfully identified her big butt.

Like Tara, Judy also needed to identify her big butt to discern what was holding her back from finding a more fulfilling position. Judy was an elementary school teacher. For many years she loved her work, but for the past couple of years she has felt a longing to interact with older, more mature students. She would love to go back to school and get a doctorate degree so that she could teach at the university level but has not allowed herself to follow her passion.

Judy had a troubling childhood. Her mother became ill when Judy was only eight years old and consequently succumbed to a crippling depression. Eventually she passed away. Her father was preoccupied with raising his children and trying to earn a living. For as long as Judy can remember, she has felt a void in her life and concluded that the lack of a female role model has rendered her ill equipped to be a role model for other girls.

It was eye opening for Judy when she realized that she could pursue her coveted doctorate, if she thought she would be a good role model. Her big butt was her belief that her childhood rendered her inadequate to work with older students. "I could work in a university," she realized, "if only I was a good role model." Now, having identified her big butt, she could finally move forward. She could stop allowing her big butt to control her future path.

Some Big Butts are Harder to Find than Others

For most of us, it is not too difficult to identify our big butts. We are painfully reminded about what we don't like about ourselves every time we look in the mirror or hear that voice shouting in our ear, "You're not smart enough, verbal enough, or whatever enough." When our flaws make themselves known, or when we can easily discern them by asking ourselves the aforementioned questions, we have taken the first step toward accepting and dismantling their control over our lives.

Sometimes, however, we have tried hiding our big butts from the world for so hard and for so long, that they have become invisible even to ourselves. Rather than simply knowing that we feel inadequate because of a soft bulging stomach, discolored facial splotch, or lack of sophistication, we instead, just experience an amorphous feeling of insecurity and lack of confidence. Harriet is a case in point.

Harriet works in health care. She has a small cubicle and has spent the last six years in virtual isolation. She is a people person and hates the thought of going to work and spending eight hours in her "cage." By all accounts, Harriet is an extremely attractive, well-educated woman. She has received strong yearly reviews and is very good at what she does.

"I could talk to my boss about a change in my environment or perhaps a move to another, more lively department," she admitted, "but I just don't have enough confidence." She does not know why she feels incompetent and inadequate. In other words, there was not a specific flaw she could articulate to help her identify her big butt. At least she was finally truthful in admitting to herself that her insecurities were stopping her. Once she could see that *she* was stopping herself, she could proceed to identify what was causing her poor self-image, what was her big butt.

For Harriet, and those like her, who know they feel insecure and lack confidence, but can't identify their big butt, the following may be helpful:

- For one week record your negative self-talk. In other words, anytime you hear that inner voice saying why you can't do something or why you do not measure up, stop and record the message. You should soon determine a pattern.

- Talk to a close friend and ask them if they have any clue as to what is keeping you from being more confident in yourself.

- On a piece of paper, describe the attributes of someone you admire. The following day, on another sheet of paper, describe yourself. Compare the two sheets to see if you can determine where you think you fall short.

- Ask yourself, what characteristics about myself would I not want to see in my children?

- Consider seeking help from a mental health professional to determine the cause of your feelings of inadequacy and to identify your big butt.

Whether your big butt is easily discernible, or whether it's become hidden over time, your goal is to label that which is blocking your path. By seeing and naming the obstruction, you give yourself the freedom to move forward with your life. You force yourself to make a conscious decision to either remain stifled because of your vulnerabilities, or to learn how to accept them and keep them from impeding your journey. Do you want to continue allowing your big butt to control you, or is it time for you to stop missing opportunities and thwarting your chances for true success and happiness?

Chapter Three

IS YOUR BIG BUTT EVEN BIGGER THAN YOU THINK?

UP UNTIL THE POINT WHEN I FINALLY ACCEPTED MY OWN BIG BUTT, I had allowed it to completely define me and stop me from pursuing my dreams. I was not able to escape from the burden of carrying around those extra pounds of flesh and shame. I've since found that while some women, like me, are only too aware of how their big butts control their personal and professional lives, others are oblivious to its damages. Make no mistake though. These big butts are dangerous! The sooner you come to understand what havoc they are wreaking on your life, the sooner you can dismantle their power and begin your journey to success.

Sometimes the costs of trying to hide our big butts can be easily calculated. How much time and money do we spend trying to camouflage our physical flaws? From cosmetic surgery to total body reconstruction, we yearn to hide what we hate and add what we're missing. Yet, few of us achieve satisfaction by these methods. Even if our big butts are surgically reduced, they remain large in our minds. How many of us willingly wear a bathing suit in public? How many times have we turned down an invitation to a party or networking event because we were having a bad-hair day or because an uninvited pimple appeared on our face? How many of us think more about how we *look* when we're presenting a report than about *what* we are presenting?

Other costs of hiding our big butts are more insidious and more damaging than missing out on a single networking event or squandering a few thousand dollars on liposuction. By blaming, protecting, camouflaging, overcompensating, or apologizing for our big butts, we are sabotaging our personal and career paths.

When we do not like or accept a part of ourselves, it is natural to cope by either trying to hide it from others and even ourselves, or to overcompensate for its existence. We may not even realize we are doing this. It is crucial however, that we become painfully aware of the full detrimental effect protecting our big butts may have on our careers, our relationships, on our whole lives. We must acknowledge the amount of time and energy we have wasted on our imperfections and refuse to give our big butts one more ounce of power.

But first, let's take a closer look at exactly how we let our big butts rule our lives. To be clear, I am not a psychologist, psychiatrist, or social worker. Rather, I have worked with, studied, mentored and motivated women my entire adult life. From the dressing room to the boardroom, I've observed women unknowingly attempt to cope with their insecurities, their big butts, by engaging in behavior that is detrimental to their well-being and success. I've classified these behaviors into seven categories:

1. The Needy

2. The Non-Promoter

3. The Tyrant

4. The Avoider

5. The Perfectionist

6. The Egotist

7. The Pleaser

These categories are by no means inclusive, and aspects of some behaviors overlap with others. At the end of each category section below is a list of questions to help you determine if your behavior is similar to that described. I am not asking you to keep score, as we all probably share some aspects of each behavior pattern. What I am asking you to do is to understand the full cost of protecting your big butt. Then, make the decision that the cost is too high—you are no longer willing to pay the price.

1. The Needy

Our insecurities frequently push us to become overly reliant on praise and validation from others. Feeling inadequate on the inside because of our big butts, we rely on outside reinforcement to build our self-esteem. We are relentless in our quest for stroking, but stroking never brings complete satisfaction because of our insatiable appetite. Even when we do get compliments, we dismiss them as meaningless, or inconsequential. We are always searching for more because there can never be enough positive words to fill the void we feel inside, to remove our big butts.

For example, with bated breath, we may ask our partner, "Does this dress make me look fat?" Regardless of their answer, we continue to try on numerous outfits. "Which one is the most slenderizing?" we continue to sheepishly inquire. We may or may not go with their selection. Either way, once we are dressed and arrive at our destination, we still grab a girlfriend and run to the nearest ladies room mirror for additional confirmation.

Scanning our environment, desperate for compliments, nothing is off limits. We show off our possessions and boast about our skills. We may offer tours of our homes or reel off the accomplishments of our children. We anxiously wait for someone to notice our new car, or flashy jewelry. We urgently urge others to taste our cooking. "Have you tried *my* dip?" Or, "I made the carrot cake." We brag about our latest travels or tournaments.

Our neediness, while simply annoying to those at home, may have devastating consequences in the workplace. When I worked with Tammy, she was a paralegal. She saw herself as inadequate because she perceived that some concepts did not come quite as quickly to her as to other people. She confided in me that she felt like she "was playing a role that she could not fulfill." This lack of confidence in her intelligence was Tammy's big butt. Even though Tammy was able to identify her insecurities, she was not aware of the full cost of protecting them. She knew she felt intellectually deficient, but she didn't realize that she tried to make up for her perceived shortcomings by becoming overly dependent on external verification for validation of her work product. While she did receive some praise, it was never enough. She desperately desired a gold star after each project and interpreted a lack of compliments from her boss as a negative reflection on her work.

This inaccurate interpretation began a chain reaction as her feeling of incompetence grew. For Tammy, the final straw was a department meeting, where a co-worker was singled out for praise on a large case, but there was no mention of Tammy's contribution. Unable to handle her self-imposed diagnosis, that she was not good enough, she actually handed in her resignation as an offensive move to avoid being fired. The irony was that her boss was extremely pleased with Tammy's work. He was shocked at receiving her notice. Admittedly, he could have been better at positive reinforcement, she should have also been lauded at the departmental meeting; but in the end, it was Tammy's insecurities, her big butt, that caused her to lose her job.

Whether we're at home or at work, we all like compliments. However, if you find yourself consistently trying to impress others or looking to the reactions of others as a reflection on your own value, this may signal that your vulnerabilities are speaking louder than your competencies. Go to your space and ask yourself the following questions. Too many affirmative answers indicate that your big butt is bigger than you think!

- Do I often try to impress others?

- Do I brag a lot, or show off?

- Do I spend a lot of energy trying to get compliments?

- Do I think there is something wrong if I do not get positive reinforcement?

- Do I interpret no response as a negative response?

- Do I trust my judgments of myself?

2. The Non-Promoter

Our big butts may cause us to refrain from expressing ourselves with confidence or keep us from going after what we want with determination. Unlike the women who seek out praise by bragging, and by searching for compliments, some of us deal with our vulnerabilities by trying to remain in the background and not calling attention to ourselves. In trying to hide our big butts, we end up hiding our strengths and talents.

I've sat in too many meetings and around too many boardroom tables, listening to the silence of women afraid to put themselves out on a limb. In everything from our body language to the seat we choose around the table, we may, without even realizing it, project an image of weakness. Similarly, when we fail to assert ourselves or speak hesitantly, overusing qualifiers (such as maybe, perhaps, possibly, conceivably), we are perceived as lacking confidence. We may overly prepare, check and double check our facts, and triple check our sources. Then, even when we are certain of how to proceed, we mumble out, "perhaps this might work," rather, than proclaiming, "yes, let's do it!"

Along the same lines, I've heard far too many women dismiss compliments and refuse to take full credit for their work. I cringe when I hear a woman diminishing the value of her efforts. I'm referring to statements like, "Oh, it wasn't a big deal. I had a lot of help," rather than, "Thank you. I'm proud of it also."

We are perceived the way we present. We certainly do not show strength if we cannot proffer opinions, accept compliments, and take full credit for our work and efforts. We need to be our own best advocates. Employers look to promote and hire those who demonstrate and inspire confidence and competence. As the old saying goes, "Perception is reality." We must convey an image of strength by speaking proudly of our accomplishments. Unfortunately, this is almost impossible to accomplish when we are terrified that someone will see our big butt and conclude that we are frauds. Perhaps nowhere is this more evident than during a job interview.

Jennifer was a recent business school graduate seeking a job in the finance department of a midsized corporation. She graduated in the top twenty percent of her class from an excellent school. Despite her success, she went through life comparing herself to an older sister who had graduated top in her class. Jennifer's big butt was her erroneous belief that her comparatively lower class rank rendered her inadequate. "Tell me, how you did you do in school?" her prospective employer queried. "Not great," she replied. "I really wanted to be in the top ten percent of our class, but I did very poorly in marketing and tax. This brought my GPA down. I'm sorry."

Contrast the interview with Jennifer to that of Megan. Megan attended the same school and was also in the top twenty percent of her class. "So, how did you do in school?" she was asked. "Great!" she replied. "I was able to graduate in the top twenty percent of my class while also participating in numerous extracurricular activities like student government." It is not difficult to guess who got the job.

I've interviewed multitudes of women, like Jennifer, who have credentials equal to or better than other applicants, yet they minimize their accomplishments and in so doing diminish their perceived value. Their big butts keep them from extolling their virtues; they are their own worst enemy.

The unwillingness to self-promote may be fatal to your career when it keeps you from aggressively seeking new, influential business relationships. As we will discuss in length in Part II, the key to success in the workplace is the ability to form connections and develop the relationships integral to helping you reach your goals. In almost every industry, the woman who can bring in business will prosper. Likewise, in the nonprofit arena the woman who can raise money and form influential connections will thrive. Our big butts may be responsible for our unwillingness to self-promote and our lack of assertiveness in going after those essential contacts. When we already feel unworthy, we are loathe to put ourselves in an even more vulnerable positions by handing out business cards, asking potential clients for meetings, attending networking events, and engaging in other integral outreach strategies.

Rather than seeking opportunities to advance your career or yourself, are you spending your energy trying to be inconspicuous and hiding your big butt? Return to your space and ask yourself the following questions:

- If appropriate, do I hesitate to sit at the head of the table?

- Am I reluctant to give an opinion?

- Do I refuse to take full credit for my efforts?

- Do I diminish compliments?

- Do I refrain from standing up tall and projecting strength when entering a room?

- Do I present my accomplishments by focusing on the negative?

- Do I neurotically apologize for everything?

- Do I hesitate to hand out business cards?

- Am I reluctant to attend networking opportunities?

- Do I create excuses to not ask potential clients for meetings?

3. The Tyrant

Women are certainly in a double bind. If we are too passive we are seen as incompetent, yet if we're too aggressive we may be labeled bitchy. Realistically, either extreme may be detrimental to our success and we want to make sure that we do not fall on the far end of either spectrum because of our big butts.

What is too aggressive? On my measuring stick, if it's appropriate for a man, it's appropriate for a woman. I applaud the woman who asserts herself in an appropriate manner. For purposes of this section, I am addressing the woman who is outright domineering. I'm thinking Meryl Streep in *The Devil Wears Prada*. You know, the woman who is totally domineering and controlling, demanding 24/7 attention to her every need. That type of clearly overly aggressive behavior, is often symptomatic of overcompensating for feelings of inadequacy—a big butt. Ever heard of a "Napoleon Complex"? That's what I am referring to here.

Specifically, I'm talking about those of us who have a take no prisoners approach to hiding our big butts. In an attempt to shield that which we dislike about ourselves, we build a fortress so that the enemy cannot attack. The enemy is defined as anyone who tries to penetrate our wall by questioning our actions, challenging our conclusions, or exposing our flaws. To protect ourselves we come off as mean and aggressive. We are so afraid that our real selves might be exposed, that we show no vulnerabilities. Unfortunately, this type of behavior works to repel, rather than attract, friends, colleagues, and clients.

When I think of someone who overcompensates for her feelings of inadequacy, I can't help but think about a former beauty queen, Carol. Her big butt is the fact that she is getting older and has not aged gracefully. She spends her time fighting against nature, trying to cover up the telltale signs of aging. While her time spent with her plastic surgeons is escalating, her relationships are faltering. Trying to overcompensate for her lost youthful appearance, her big butt, she has become demanding and demeaning. Carol is an industrial consultant. She has been known to shout orders to her employees, often reducing those under her supervision to tears. Her world revolves around her and she has lost the ability to look at things through others' eyes. In trying to keep from exposing her age, she has instead exposed an unlikeable persona and cut herself off from meaningful relationships.

Are you protecting your big butt by overcompensating to the point where you are tyrannical? Ask yourself these questions.

- Do I become furious when criticized?

- Do I always have to have the last word?

- Do I try to put others down rather than building them up?

- Do I disregard others' feelings in my communications?

- Do I get defensive when questioned?

4. The Avoider

Another way we protect our big butts is by avoiding change and responsibility. Simply put, once we've landed in a place of relative safety, we are afraid to move for fear that our big butt might be exposed. We know we can handle where we are, we are currently able to maintain the status quo without divulging our flaws, why risk moving to higher ground?

This fear of change can manifest itself in numerous ways. We may be reluctant to leave toxic relationships, change our living environment, look for different employment, or seek new adventure. We will not risking leaving the known, as the unknown may expose our big butt.

Beatrice had spent almost a decade on Wall Street before she made the decision to stay home and raise her children. They have all been out of the house for many years, and Beatrice finds her life purposeless and boring. Having been out of the job market for so long, she knows she will have to brush up on her computer skills to land meaningful employment. Her lack of ability in essential skills such as compiling Excel spreadsheets and formatting PowerPoint presentations is her big butt. Yet, she refuses to even consider exposing it by taking the classes offered at the local community college to ready her for the workforce.

Over coffee I suggested she look into another industry. As a talented, articulate, and bright woman there are many doors open for her. Nevertheless, she has a reason to reject every possible solution. All of her excuses have one thing in common: she is afraid of change because of her lack of ability in computer skills, her big butt.

Sometimes, we are so adverse to change that we may even sabotage our careers by turning down promotions or other opportunities for advancement. Many years ago I was in the children's clothing business. One of our best employees was Maria. Maria was happy to show up an hour before we opened at 10 a.m. and stay for an hour after we closed at 9 p.m. She was a fabulous salesperson and great with all the other demanding details from ringing the register to getting new stock out in a timely manner. It only made sense that we offer Maria a raise and ask her to become an assistant manager.

She flatly turned down the promotion. I couldn't believe it, "But, Maria," I exclaimed. "You are working the hours anyway and you will make significantly more money."

Adamantly shaking her head, she responded, "I really do not want the responsibility." There was no changing her mind. Through the years, as I came to know Maria better, it became clear, that her big butt was her fear of numbers; she hated math. She had wrongly convinced herself that if she accepted the new title she would be required to intricately understand the store's finances. These phantom expectations were an overreaction to her vulnerability.

Through the years I've come across many women who chose to turn down the opportunity for advancement, in spite of the fact that they were already performing duties will beyond their job descriptions. Their insecurities keep them from assuming a bigger title, taking on more responsibilities, or learning additional skills. Is your big butt keeping you tied to the status quo in your personal or professional life? Ask yourself these questions:

- Do I avoid change for no apparent reason?

- Am I afraid if I move up in my career I will appear incompetent?

- Do I maintain toxic relationships because something is better than nothing?

- Do I have interests I'd like to pursue but I'm afraid that I might fail?

- Do I invent excuses for not moving forward in my life?

5. The Perfectionist

Unlike those of us who avoid taking on more responsibility, the perfectionist will move forward but with much angst, because anything she does must be carried out with the highest standards of excellence. "Good enough" is a foreign concept. Perfectionists neurotically obsess over the simplest task, because it has to be completed impeccably.

Those of us who are perfectionists do not easily distinguish between what really requires scrutiny from what really doesn't matter. We put tremendous pressure on ourselves to meet impossible standards. Consequently, simple projects become monumental tasks because it is so much work to meet our self-imposed standards. Our friends, families, and employers learn to shield us from obligations because it is too tiring and painful for them to deal with our anxiety.

We avoid criticism at all costs; yet, ironically, we are our own biggest critic. We tend to justify our actions ad nauseam; anything to evade negative judgment. In other words, similarly to the tyrant, we must be impeccable on the outside because we feel so flawed on the inside. While the tyrant tries to compensate for her big butt by acting overly aggressive, the perfectionist puts unrealistic expectations upon herself. Carol, a middle-aged hotel manager, is a typical example.

Five years ago, after seventeen years of marriage, Carol's husband left her for a younger woman. Unable to see his own way out of a full-blown midlife crisis, he jumped ship. His abandonment reinforced what Carol has long been trying to protect: her belief that she is unattractive, her big butt. Admittedly, she does have a rather long face, big teeth and a wide jaw. She painfully remembers a schoolmate calling her "horse's mouth." Since that time, she has spent much of her life experimenting with different makeup techniques and hairstyles trying to cover up her imperfections. She deals with her facial flaws by making certain everything else she does is flawless.

Carol knows that she's a perfectionist, but defends her actions declaring, "If it's worth doing it's worth doing right." While this may be true, Carol's "right" reaches unprecedented heights. For example, this past November was her turn to host Thanksgiving. For many years Carol tried to avoid hosting, but had run out of excuses. It is important to note that she is not lazy. She is anything but lazy. It's just that her definition of "right" was extraordinarily difficult for anyone to achieve.

In April, seven months before the big event, Carol began taking measures to make sure her home was meticulous. She replaced shrubs on the outside and a sofa on the inside. She had her carpets cleaned and her windows scoured. She even bought new dishes with a harvest theme trim. Then she turned her attention, her fixation, on the menu, accompanied by an endless pile of recipes.

If this was fun for Carol, I wouldn't use her as an example, but, on the contrary, she made herself and her family nuts. On about the fiftieth call to her sister she asks, "Do you think I need both baked sweet potatoes and a sweet potato casserole?"

A few minutes later, "How many different vegetables should I make? Do you think most people will eat this artichoke and spinach soufflé or should I add that green-bean casserole topped with onion rings?"

No one is immune to her quest for perfection as she calls her brother and grills him about the wine. "Should I leave the wine glasses at the bar, or put one at each place setting? Do I need separate glasses for the white and red or can one size do for both?"

Her angst trumped the joy of the holiday. She placed more meaning on serving the perfect meal in the perfect setting than she did on the meaning of the holiday and the company of her parents, siblings, and children.

Women, who are perfectionists like Carol, also manifest their insecurities in the workplace. Obviously, many functions do require the highest degree of precision. We are aghast at the image of a sloppy surgeon. However, the perfectionist does not differentiate and often does not prioritize or delegate. So, while the surgeon has to be precise during the operation, she does not have to insist that her paperwork be stapled horizontally, at the right hand corner, a quarter of an inch from the top of the paper!

Are you so afraid of exposing your big butt that you need to control your environment to an unrealistic degree of perfection? Is this hampering your success? Ask yourself these questions:

- Do I obsess over every detail, even if it doesn't matter?

- Am I afraid to delegate because no one can do it as well as I can?

- Do I consistently check even my simplest work three and even four times?

- Do projects seem to consume me more than they do other people?

- Do I think it's never OK to be sloppy?

- Would I be unduly embarrassed if my shirt has a slight stain?

6. The Egotist

I've known Martha, a close friend's relative, for over twenty years. It recently occurred to me that in all these years she has never given me a compliment. In fact, I can't remember ever hearing her say something nice about anyone other than herself. Martha is so consumed with protecting her own big butt that she has no space left to think about or empathize with others. Simply put, her world revolves around her. She thinks of herself first, second, and third. Martha's big butt is money. She grew up extremely poor, sharing a bedroom with three siblings. Her wardrobe consisted of hand-me downs, and she recalls spending many nights unable to sleep because she was hungry. Even though she now lives a financially stable life, she allows her past impoverishment, her big butt, to make her feel inadequate.

Martha is not a mean woman; just self-involved. She needs to portray herself as the ultimate authority on every subject, and you can be sure if you have a story to tell, she will have one that is funnier, scarier, sadder, or more interesting. She will throw you under the bus, if she thinks it will make her look good. In other words, she needs to make herself look more, by making others look less. She becomes jealous often because she is threatened so easily.

Women like Martha, whose biggest concern is protecting their own egos, will not reach out to others if there is a chance that they may be judged or rejected in the process. As one woman sheepishly confessed, she would spend a Saturday night home alone, rather than calling a friend to go out, thereby confirming she had no plans on a Saturday night. Likewise, she admitted that she will not ask for friends on Facebook because they may not accept.

Like the women relying on external validation or overcompensating to cover up their big butts, egocentric women need the conversation to revolve around them. They may ask how you're doing, but really aren't listening; instead they are waiting for you to finish so that they can talk about themselves. You remember the old line, "I've talked enough about me, now let's hear what you think about me!" In fact, the only time they seem to light up is when they successfully steer the conversation back to themselves.

Egocentric women can be a nightmare in the workplace or at committee meetings. They frequently interrupt, unable to wait to share their ideas. They do not really listen to the comments of others, as they are solely concerned with expressing their own, superior, position. Thus, they usually manage to prolong meetings, frequently repeating ideas in their own words, to ensure that they receive the credit.

It is difficult to form friendships or good business connections if you are so consumed with protecting your vulnerabilities and proving your legitimacy that you have nothing left to give to others. By working so hard to protect you and your big butt, you are in reality, pushing others away. Your behavior is repelling the very relationships you are seeking. Do the following statements apply to you?

- Do I get bored listening to others?

- Do I like nothing better than impressing other people?

- Do I find myself frequently interrupting?

- Do I know much about the families of my closest co-workers?

- Do I find it unimportant to keep track of other people's birthdays?

- Do I refrain from initiating social interactions?

7. The Pleaser

The pleasers try blending into the background but they are easy to spot. They have so little respect for themselves that they allow others to take advantage and walk all over them. They have difficulty saying no. They usually smile, but there is no joy in their eyes. They will go to any lengths to please and have difficulty setting limits. Like the women in our other categories, pleasers define themselves in terms of their big butts. Because they do not like themselves, they mistakenly conclude that they are not worthy of consideration and respect. They view themselves as nonentities.

Tamara was a pleaser. She hated herself for being over-weight, her big butt. She amplified the effects of her extra pounds by neglecting her personal appearance. She felt she was unworthy of nice clothes, new hairstyles, manicures, and facials. In her mind, she physically took up so much space, that she desperately needed to recoil from any further attention. Rather, she deemed herself only worthy of serving others. At home, her children would volunteer her as the weekend driver and frequently ask her to bring forgotten lunches and home-work to school. Her husband took her for granted and used his passive-aggressive nature to test her and see if she would set limits. He would travel on business to exotic destinations, but never ask her to go. He would stay out late entertaining clients, leaving her home with the children. He bought himself expensive cars and jewelry, yet she got nothing. The more she tolerated his disrespect and mistreatment, the more it esca-lated. Her discounting of herself set the standard for how oth-ers, even her husband, perceived her.

In the workplace, it was no different. She was the one ev-eryone expected to assume the unpleasant tasks and boring assignments. Basically, she was the office doormat. Sadly, she never complained and was never promoted. She had effec-tively convinced herself and others that her big butt rendered her worthless.

Of all the behavior patterns we have discussed, the pleaser is the saddest. The one who fits this category is unable to es-cape the confines of her big butt and has allowed it to com-pletely define her. Are you a pleaser?

- Do you have difficulty saying no?

- Do you often feel resentful?

- Do you allow yourself to be mistreated?

- Do you find yourself volunteering and then asking why?

- Do you have difficulty asserting yourself?

- Do you try not to call attention to yourself?

As you can see, our attempts to hide our big butts are causing us to be the kind of people we do not want to be. What are the unintended ramifications of your own big butt? How is your big butt causing you to act and how do those actions keep you from enjoying your life to the fullest? Does it hamper your personal, social, and professional relationships? Can you imagine all you could enjoy and accomplish if you rendered your big butt impotent?

Chapter Four

ARE YOU READY TO DECLARE YOUR BIG BUTT IMPOTENT?

WE HAVE NOW IDENTIFIED OUR BIG BUTTS AND SEEN JUST HOW large a role they may play in sabotaging our lives. Armed with this information, we have a choice. We can either continue to allow them to block our paths, or we can accept them for what they are and move on to accept the awards that life and work have waiting for us.

While on the surface, this seems an easy choice, when it comes time to actually take the plunge, we may experience some pullback. Change is difficult, especially when it requires us to neutralize what we previously viewed with disdain. It also takes us out of our comfort zones. Let's face it—even though our big butts are holding us back, they have controlled us for so long that we fear the consequences of letting them go.

To move on we must convince ourselves completely and unequivocally that we are worthy of more and deserve to be free. Once we are free from their control, we will have to take full responsibility for ourselves and our actions. We will no longer be able to use our big butts as the excuse for not moving forward.

We Deserve More

One of the most sinister effects of allowing our big butt to define us is that over time, such thinking may whittle away at our self-worth. We may begin to believe that we do not deserve to be or achieve more; we have landed in the only place where we are entitled to be. How dare we settle for less! Yet, after spending a lifetime despising a part of ourselves, it is no wonder that our self-image is diminished.

We are the only ones who can give ourselves power. The strength and determination must come from within. While friends and family may revel in our joys and empathize with our sorrows, at the end of the day, we are the ones in control, the only ones who can grab the reins of our lives and move on.

Too many of us have actually convinced ourselves that we have no choice. Our self-esteem has been so decimated that we cannot see past the boundaries of our big butts. This is our lot in life and we just have to accept it. What a shame, what a waste not to live our lives to the fullest. How sad to allow our perceived flaws to keep us from sharing our gifts with the world. Before we can move on and achieve our dreams, we must choose to believe that we deserve to be all that we can be.

Annabelle is a case in point. She is a well-educated woman who put her professional goals aside to help her husband achieve his potential. She ran the household, raised the children, and generally managed their lives in the traditional sense. Now that her kids have grown, Annabelle feels empty. Yet, she tells herself that she has no right to demand more from her life. As her husband's successful career has given her great financial rewards, she feels she is being selfish in now seeking her own, personal satisfaction.

She knows that her big butt is her general insecurity over her lack of experience in the world. She explains, "All I really know is how to manage a house and take care of children. I have neither the skills nor sophistication to get out there and find out who I really am. I am stuck. I look at all these other women who seem to effortlessly navigate their broader environment, and then there's me." By convincing herself of her inadequacies, she confines her life to the borders defined by her role as mother and homemaker. Yet, she is so unhappy. She has not given herself permission to accept her big butt and move on.

The bottom line is that on some level, she does not feel she deserves more. As she succinctly states, "I really shouldn't complain. Most women would give their right arm to live my life. I have a beautiful home and Jim provides me with anything I want. There must be something wrong with me. I have no right to be unhappy."

On the contrary, what right does she have to waste one precious moment not maximizing her natural gifts? Annabelle needed to make a conscious decision to either spend her days on the edge of the diving board, never jumping in, or taking a deep breath, accepting who she was, and plunging into the wonderful sea of life.

To her credit, Annabelle chose to jump. She moved from her home planted deep within suburbia, to an exciting downtown apartment. She is taking classes, trying new hobbies, and developing a broader circle of friends.

She decided her big butt was not going to stop her from learning, doing, and experiencing her life; she did indeed deserve more.

EXERCISE – Before you embark on the process of rendering your big butt impotent, it is important for you to spend time in your space and ask yourself: Do I believe I am worthy and deserve to be more?

Taking Away Our Big Butt's Power: The Fear Factor

If we are brutally honest with ourselves, we may admit that we are reluctant to give up blaming our big butt for our unhappiness. By giving it up, we can no longer hold it responsible for keeping us back: the responsibility shifts to ourselves, and that can be scary. We've all known people who have lost a lot of weight and just as quickly put it back on. One reason for this is that when they have trimmed their big butts, they can no longer blame them for the other unhappiness in their lives. As one contestant from a widely viewed weight-loss program admitted, "It was just too much pressure not to blame my fat self for my lack of business success."

Evelyn was paralyzed in her career life. She went from job to job never really motivated to succeed and blamed her dysfunctional upbringing—her big butt. Finally, her parents convinced her to undergo family therapy. She came to realize that her childhood was not appreciably different from that of her successful siblings. No, her parents weren't perfect, but they loved her and had her best interests in mind throughout her childhood years. During an especially emotional session she inadvertently blurted out, "But, if they're not to blame then I have to blame myself!"

Like Evelyn, Donna also clung to her big butt; her conviction that she was a loser. Donna sold insurance and while she would spend an inordinate amount of time preparing proposals for prospective clients, at the first sign of rejection she would back away. "I lost another sale," she would whine, reinforcing her own dysfunctional belief that she was indeed a loser. If she weren't a loser, she would have to withstand rejection and be persistent in her follow-up. She would have to simultaneously have many balls in the air so that some would land. However, her fallback, that she was a loser, gave her permission to give up and continue as a failure. Confirming her inadequacies, became more important to her than being successful and making things happen. She could then spend her time feeling sorry for herself, convinced that she was a victim. In a perverse way, this gave her satisfaction.

EXERCISE – Go to your space and give thought to why you are holding on to your big butt. What is it doing for you? If you were to give up blaming it for your limitations—who then has the power? Can you accept this? What benefits are you getting from relying on your big butt to keep you from being all you can be?

When Your Big Butt Is Simply Too Big

It is important to note here, that the purpose of this book is to help you learn to accept, and later, use to your advantage, your vulnerabilities, your big butt. We have defined big butts as either the physical or intangible traits that we do not like about ourselves. As examples, we have looked at fat thighs, sagging breasts, large noses, and frizzy hair. We have also looked at lack of sophistication, guilt, lack of education, and other metaphorical big butts. All of these big butts are rather benign traits, not major impediments, which we must learn to accept in order to move on.

There are other more lethal traits that may pose serious danger to either ourselves or those around us. I'm talking about addictions, abuse, and other unacceptable behaviors. It is not the purpose of this book to address such behaviors or pathologies and I am not including them in our definition of big butt as they must be addressed by appropriate professionals.

It's also important to distinguish our big butts, and their accompanying consequences, from simple bad habits or ignorant behaviors. For example, as discussed in the preceding chapter, your big butt may cause you to overcompensate. However, if overcompensation includes incessant interrupting, you can modify this annoying habit while, at the same time, learning to be aware that your overcompensation may be a ramification of protecting your big butt. Again, this book addresses accepting and using our big butts to our advantage. Changing destructive behaviors and habits is outside of the scope of this book and should be addressed otherwise.

Chapter Five

ACCEPTING YOUR BIG BUTT

YOU HAVE IDENTIFIED YOUR BIG BUTT AND THE TOXIC CONSE-quences of protecting it. You also understand why it may be challenging to disengage from its hold. It is now the time for you to finally accept your imperfections and move on with your life.

I stumbled into self-acceptance through a series of inadvertent, yet enlightening discoveries, which led to the growing realization that I was living by a dysfunctional set of values. My developing awareness demanded that I examine and ultimately reject my belief system. Ultimately, to move on with my life, and to achieve my full potential, I had to accept my big butt. Now, seemingly a lifetime later, I can share my personal soul-saving insights with you to help you through your own journey to acceptance. The following seven insights helped me accept my flaws. After each insight is an exercise to help you accept your own big butt.

1. Our Big Butts Have No Inherent Power

Trying to hide from my big butt, I avoided mirrors and cameras like the plague. In my mind, my flaws were so big that the last thing I needed was objective confirmation. By never allowing myself to take a good look at my big butt or fat thighs, I allowed them to grow to monstrous proportions. To further fuel their importance, I labeled them with every negative adjective in my vocabulary: disgusting, disgraceful, hideous, fat, ugly, revolting, nauseating, and repulsive. They not only flourished, they eventually took over my life.

And then, one day, I came across a picture of myself as a child. In my head, I recalled a girl who was disgustingly obese and so ashamed. As I looked at the picture objectively, I was able to see a cute little girl. Yes, she had a visible tummy and yes she was a little round. But she also had a sweet smile and that curly hair was adorable. Sadly, she was me, and I had wasted decades being miserable because I had labeled her as fat, ugly, and unacceptable.

Continuing through my box of photos, I came across my wedding picture. Instantly, I flashed back to that day when I walked down the aisle. Rather than sparkling with a radiant smile, I was embarrassed and apologetic, cringing over my fat appearance. Now, seeing the bride with new lenses, she was beautiful. Yes, she was a little chubby, but, so what?

My search escalated. Sifting through boxes and boxes of photos, I frantically sought affirmation of my newfound awareness. There I was at my third- grade birthday party, there I was at the beach during a family vacation in Hawaii; and there was my stomach, butt, thighs, frizzy hair, and hips. But they had no inherent power. Their only power emanated from me.

It is time for you to stop those disparaging thoughts and accept that your big butt is what it is and nothing more. Once

you've learned to neutralize your attitude toward your imperfections, you will be able to accept them.

If your big butt is a physical feature, you might want to
take a picture of it, or stand in front of a mirror. Now, while
looking directly at your nemesis, emotionally detach. Look at
it objectively as if it were the first time you ever saw it. I want
you to really look at those sagging breasts or chunky calves
without attaching any emotion to them. The minute you start
dramatizing over them-stop! Now, take a deep breath and
look again. It is often helpful to pretend the flaw belongs to
someone else. Imagine those ears on someone you love. Now,
try seeing them on someone you do not even know. In other
words, just look at your blemishes, like a child discovering a
new object for the first time, seeing them with no preconcep-
tion, no judgment, simply with wonder and awe. Describe your
big butt in objective terms; no negative adjectives allowed!

By taking part in this exercise, Heather, for the first time,
looked objectively at her wrinkles. Up until now she could not
even glance at them without stressing out because she had
concluded that their existence meant she was too old for new
beginnings. Really seeing them objectively, she described
what she saw. "I see two folds in my skin running from the middle of my nose going downward to my mouth like an inverted
"v." They are not very deep. When I smile they disappear. I also
see three lines going horizontally across my forehead."

For Heather, a light bulb went on; she realized that her
wrinkles were simply a pattern on her face — nothing more.
They did not have any power. It was what she told herself about
them that gave them power, the adjectives she attached to

them. When she labeled them as "ugly and disgusting," they were. It was the labels, not the wrinkles, that mattered. Seeing them just as wrinkles took away their power.

If your big butt is an intangible, you can confront it in a similar fashion by objectively looking at it. While you cannot take a physical picture of guilt or internal feelings of inadequacy, you can write down exactly what you identify as your big butt. Describe it without adjectives. Like we did with the physical big butt, sometimes it's helpful to pretend it belongs to someone else so that you have the ability to distance yourself when describing it.

Katherine worked at an upscale salon in downtown Chicago. Her secret goal was to own her own salon, but her lack of education, her big butt, kept her from pursuing her dreams. Rather than seeing herself as a work in process, she had labeled herself as uneducated and stupid. By writing down and describing her big butt in objective terms, "I attended one year of college. That was what I could manage at the time." She was able to remove the discriminating adjectives and just see herself as someone who had not finished school.

It's ironic how we can accept and even love the flaws of our friends and family. We can see our son's double chin as cute or our best friend's cellulite as benign. Yet, those same imperfections are intolerable if they belong to us. Again, our big butts have no inherent power; it's what we tell ourselves about them that gives them their power.

After spending a lifetime applying negative labels to our big butts, it takes some practice to break the habit. However, by becoming mindful of your negative judgments and stopping yourself from once again going down that track, you can learn to neutralize your reaction to your flaws.

EXERCISE – For one twenty-four hour period, carry a tape recorder or notebook and record *every* negative message you tell yourself about your big butt. How many times a day do you think you are not thin enough? How many times a day do you let yourself feel guilty for working and feel the companion thought—you are not being a good mother? How many times a day do you think you are not x, y, or z enough?

Now, in the following twenty-four hours, every time you find yourself thinking negative thoughts, say ENOUGH and replace the negative judgment with, "It is what it is, nothing more. It is part of me, it does not define me."

2. How Dare I Judge Myself by Meaningless Criteria?

To be fair, I was not the only one who vilified my flaws. As I mentioned earlier, living in South Florida, it seemed that beauty and thinness were all that mattered; the skinny bitches ruled. Even if I could stop judging myself, wouldn't those around me still view me as inadequate?

I believed that unless I could lose weight, straighten my hair, get rid of my cellulite, and basically transform my physical being, I would not be accepted, and therefore, I could never be happy. I was doomed. Even if I were to lose weight, I thought I would still fall short. My legs were not long and graceful, my torso not lean and fit, my nose not cute, my features not chiseled. I would never approach the breathtaking perfection of those gorgeous, South-Florida women. I could not compete. Playing by the existing rules, I was losing, not only the game, but myself. Up until this point, it was the only competition I knew.

I tentatively began to question the validity of these standards that I so desperately wanted to meet—those artificial measures of self-worth. Fortunately, I slowly awoke to the realization that I did not have to participate in this ridiculous charade. I had the choice of accepting or rejecting what I was coming to see as meaningless criteria. It was a game I could not win—how utterly shameful to keep trying. I did not let go easily, but continued to grasp onto the destructive illusion, until I could no longer do it—until my fingers gave way. Humiliation and disgust over my appearance kept me from participating in life. I had lost myself.

It is not easy to reject a pervasive set of standards. When my family, friends, social circle, and society all seemed to be playing the same game, how dare I opt out? Who was I to declare the game fallacious? Yet, how dare I keep striving towards a goal I could not achieve? How many diets did I have to try? How many hair straightening products did I have to go through? How much longer did I need to loathe my body, my being?

I clearly remember the first time I allowed myself to question the integrity of this game. I was manager of a women's clothing store, just after college graduation. I quickly learned that the best place to capture a customer's attention, and make a sale, was when she was the most vulnerable—partially naked in the dressing room. There she stood, stripped of any barriers, sharing the tiny space with her enemy—a full length mirror. I would hand her articles of clothing that would flatter her body type, as she carefully slid the curtain to one side, leaving a space only big enough to put her hand through. I would urge her to trust my suggestions and proceed to gently coax her out of the room and guide her to the three way mirror.

I was amazed. More often than not, there was absolutely no correlation between how a customer actually looked and how she thought she looked. Reality was shunned, perception was all that mattered. "This makes by butt look too big!" a tiny, impish woman would exclaim. Another, a tall magnificent blonde, would scrutinize her perfect body in the mirror sighing, "I hate my hips." I would have given my right arm to trade my hips for hers. "I'm too short." "I'm too tall." "I'm too fat." "I'm too…" Fill in the blank. It doesn't matter. Almost all my customers seemed to think they had some unforgivable body flaw. Everybody had a big butt.

In other words, *everyone* was playing a game that nobody could win. The rules required perfection. No one could measure up, and at the end of the game everyone felt inadequate. It slowly began to occur to me, maybe there was nothing wrong with us. Maybe, something was wrong with the rules we blindly relied on to measure our self-worth?

You must consciously establish *your own* meaningful set of rules and expectations. You need to honestly figure out what really matters to you. You are the only one who has to look in that mirror and accept you. Forget trying to win the approval of others. This is an exhausting, never-ending and impossible task. The truth is that other people are really only thinking about themselves. If they even consider you, they are applying *their* standards for *their* evaluation. They look to you in measuring themselves. What other people think is almost always about them—not about you.

This concept was once again so vividly brought home to me when I attended a wedding with a group of friends. In the weeks leading up to the big event we were all focused on what we would wear, how we would do our hair, where we would get our makeup done, *etc.* The big day finally came. As I closely watched and listened to my friends it was clear—each one was self-focused; consumed with what others thought about how *they* looked. They proffered the politically correct platitudes to the other guests: "You look so nice. Where did you get that dress? I love your hair." But, if they were honest with themselves, they would admit that what they were really interested in was others' opinions of *them*.

EXERCISE – Go to your space and ask yourself:

- Am I judging myself by the superficial and ultimately meaningless criteria of others?

- What really matters to me?

- Is it happiness?

- Is it contentment and peace of mind?

- Is it being a good person?

- Is it making the world a better place?

- Is it being a supportive and good role model for my family?

The ultimate question for you to answer is: Am I judging myself by standards that are meaningful to *me*?

3. Everyone has a Big Butt either Behind Them or in Their Head

From my experience helping women in the dressing room, I began to view the world with a different lens. Witnessing the self-loathing of so many objectively attractive women, I began to realize that no one was perfect. Everyone had some type of physical flaw or other inadequacy. Instead of focusing on my own big butt, I became vigilant in detecting the self-perceived imperfections and insecurities of others, oftentimes the very ones that judged and taunted me. While my big butt and fat thighs were my personal archenemy—in reality, everyone had a big butt. Throughout my life, working with women in a wide variety of settings, this truth has been consistently reinforced. In fact, just recently I was visiting my family in Miami. A woman with legs up to my shoulders got in the elevator. She was wearing short, short, short, white shorts accompanied by a colorfully printed top. It was impossible for me not to stare at her. As she became aware of my fixation, I said, "I love your outfit, you look so beautiful." She smiled and retorted, "I love wearing this shirt, "she then grabbed a small handful of fabric and continued, "see, it blouses out and hides my stomach." Trying to contain my nausea, I wished her a good day. Miss Legs had a big butt.

As we saw in Chapter Two, in learning to identify our big butts, everyone has one. For many, like me, our big butt is literal. It is our perceived (or real) physical imperfections; large derrieres, cottage-cheese thighs, turkey necks, flat chests or whatever bodily flaw causes us to feel insecure. For others, their big butt is an intangible. It may be their fear of failure or maybe their fear of success. Perhaps it is their fear of inadequacy as a mother because they are forced to leave their child in day care. Or, maybe, it is their fear of inadequacy as an employee, for not working enough, so as not to leave their child in day care for extra hours. For many, their big butt is their belief that they are not wealthy enough, successful enough, religious enough, or educated enough. It is the overriding fear that we are simply not good enough. We become paralyzed by the thought that our secret, our big butt, will be revealed and we will be judged inadequate. Our big butt keeps us from loving ourselves and pursuing our personal goals to the fullest.

The realization that I was not alone, that I was not the only one whose self-image was decimated when defined by superficial standards, helped me to move on. The same way my literal big butt blocked my early growth, others allowed their intangible big butts to stop them dead in their tracks. The knowledge that almost everyone had some type of insecurity, based on their perceived inadequacies, gave me the strength and courage to begin reframing my own flawed self-image.

Knowing that everyone has something that they do not like about themselves, their big butts, will help you to accept your own imperfections. To help you gain this insight, keenly observe the people that you come in contact with and try to ascertain their vulnerabilities. To detect physical big butts, look at how they dress and how they carry themselves. You will find a wide assortment of various perceived imperfections such as large hips, chubby knock knees, elephant ears, and graying roots. You will also notice people trying to hide their flaws using every trick in the book from whitening their teeth and straitening their hair to lifting and enhancing their breasts.

To ascertain those intangible big butts pay close attention to conversations and behaviors. Carefully listen to what people say as well as what they don't say. Notice their body language and how they interact with others. As we discussed in Chapter Three, some women will consistently attempt to steer the conversation to themselves, craving attention and reinforcement. Others will try to blend into the background, afraid to voice their opinion on any controversial issue. By becoming cognizant of the vulnerabilities of your friends, colleagues, and acquaintances, you will soon see that we are all simply human, we all have big butts. So, why not just accept your own?

EXERCISE − Write down the names of the first ten people that come into your mind. Now, in the next few weeks try to figure out their big butt. How many could you decipher?

4. The Women I Most Admired were Not Defined by their Big Butts

My awareness of other women progressed from noticing those around me to noticing women of real power and influence. Rather than just concentrating on magazine cover models and bikini-clad screen stars, I started focusing on who really mattered to me. Who were the women that I truly respected? Who would I most want to emulate? Who could positively impact our world in meaningful ways?

It was eye opening when I realized that the women I most admired, women such as Madeline Albright, Oprah Winfrey, and Golda Meir, were not iconic because of their physical attributes. Whether they are political leaders or business powerhouses, they are not looked up to for their magnificent bodies, high cheek bones, firm thighs, or shapely butts. It is not their flawless skin or small waistlines that make them legendary. No, they are not defined by their big butts, or other meaningless vulnerabilities. They exude confidence. They carry themselves with their heads held high when they enter a room. They speak with an air of inner peace. They do not appear to need anyone's approval. They already have the ultimate approval— their own. They accept themselves, big butts, fat thighs, and all. They know that there is not a diet, exercise plan, or type of plastic surgery that could give them what they already carry inside. What they have will never sag, age, or wrinkle.

What an enlightening realization! There was no correlation between their looks and their success; between their big butts and their accomplishments. Perhaps, I no longer needed to correlate my imperfections with my capacity for success. Maybe, I just needed acceptance, from within.

EXERCISE – Go to your space, close your eyes and think about all the women you know, living or deceased. Then think about famous women in all walks of life. Make a list of the five women you most admire and respect. Now, look at this list. How many of these women would grace the cover of *Vogue* clad in a skimpy bikini? Are any of these women "perfect"? Why do you admire them?

5. You Can Win the Prize without Playing the Game

What did I really want? What were my real goals? How would I know when I achieved them? In the end, all I really wanted was peace of mind, contentment of spirit. I blindly grasped at superficialities like a slim body and beautiful hair, thinking these were the necessary steps to obtain these feelings. I realized that I could reverse the order. If I could give myself the gift, the end prize, maybe I could forgo the obsessive addiction of trying to win superficial tokens.

Quite accidently, I stumbled into situations where I felt a sense of well-being and accomplishment. Aside from the previously referred to ad hoc baton lessons, one of my first memories of success was selling Girl Scout Cookies. I walked around my neighborhood with passion and conviction and easily convinced neighbors to buy those delicious cookies. I extolled the virtues of the succulent treats and reminded my buyers that they too could indulge in cookie fantasies, while helping a worthwhile organization. I was a leader in sales. (In the spirit of full disclosure, my sales were definitely inflated by all the boxes I personally bought and ate!)

Successfully selling Girl Scout Cookies gave me the confidence to later sell other products. From holiday greeting cards to patio furniture, I learned that I was a natural salesperson, and I felt good earning my own money. It gave me a sense of control and satisfaction. This, in turn, enabled me to expand my horizons and become a successful businesswoman and community leader.

How freeing to stop chasing a frivolous and unobtainable ideal. How liberating to realize that what I was truly searching for could be found by using my true strengths and talents. I did not need a slim butt to give me satisfaction and peace of mind! With the weight of an impossible dream lifted, I was finally free to soar.

EXERCISE – Return to your space and ask yourself the following:

- What it is that you really want?

- What are your true goals and dreams?

- What vocation or avocation could you pursue to give you a sense of accomplishment and well-being?

- What steps do you need to take to achieve this goal?

- How do you want to feel on the inside?

- How about making the decision to give yourself this feeling *now*?

6. You Do Not Have to Love It—Just Accept It and Move On

As I said earlier, it was a process to transition from chastising myself for my imperfections to actualizing myself for my strengths. During this time, I began to discover that the more success I achieved, the less attention I seemed to pay to my imperfections. Subtle changes started to occur. I spent less and less time focusing on what I was not, and much more time acting on my inner drive to succeed.

I knew I was making headway when I mustered the courage to reject the advice of a plastic surgeon. Taking one last stab at trying to transform my body, I had succumbed to the conclusion that surgery would repair what willpower could not. I could undergo a total makeover. The knife would get rid of the big butt, bulging stomach and cottage-cheese thighs.

The first appointment was for The Evaluation. Dr. Plastic's assistant handed me a string belt with a small paper triangle in the middle. With the voice of a stern school principal she instructed, "Take everything off and put this on." Obediently, I followed the command, waiting in a room basically naked, the paper triangle my only shelter.

After an eternity, or at least ten minutes, Dr. Plastic and Assistant enter the room. To enhance their visibility of my flaw-filled body, they had me step on a wooden block. Marker in hand, Dr. Plastic examined his prey, noting every fat filled crevice in solemn concentration. His communication with me was limited to silent mutterings as he walked around me snapping pictures of my fat. When he finished, Assistant instructed me to get dressed and report to his office.

In the confines of Dr. Plastic's office, he exposed the flaws of other victims. He opened the picture album that was conspicuously displayed on his table and showed me the "before" and "afters" of prior subjects. I was immediately captivated by a "before" photo of a woman with breasts that hung almost to her waist. On the next page, the same women displayed new perky peaks with an almost palpable delight. Another picture depicted a woman with and without her prominent turkey neck. Putting my hand under my own chin, my hope was steadily rising. "This could really work," I let myself believe.

At last, it was my turn. Dr. Plastic took the pictures of my paper-triangle covered body, fed them into his computer and began the process of magically magnifying (what didn't need magnification)—my bodily flaws.

Finally, he showed emotion, sounding like he won the plastic surgery lottery, as he proclaimed, "Now, with the help of imaging, you can see what you will look like once we complete several (painful) procedures." With bated breath I embraced the screen. There I appeared, minus most of the fat. Problem was, it was still me. No one would stop this modified version of me to ask for a modeling contract. Heads would not turn as I sauntered down the street. It was clear. My life would not change after subjecting my body to intense surgical procedures. There had to be a better way.

In rejecting this extreme medical procedure, I made a deliberate decision once and for all to no longer subject myself to the blind adherence of arbitrary rules. I was out of the game and won the most unexpected prize— freedom.

Let's make it clear—no, I do not love my big butt, pudgy stomach, and all my other physical flaws. However, I have come to accept that they are just a part of me, nothing more. I no longer give them power. Don't get me wrong. If Jennifer Lopez or Halle Berry asked to change bodies—I would jump! Until then, I try to look my best and do not reject the notion of cosmetic help. I prefer the numbers on the scale to be lower rather than higher, and I still look in the mirror trying to decide if what I'm wearing is slenderizing. However, I will be damned if I ever again let my physical appearances stop me or define me—never.

I am not asking you to love your wide hips, slight stammer, or flabby underarms; just to accept them. Admittedly, we would all love perfect bodies and untarnished psyches. However, we are who we are. We can never expect others to accept us if we cannot accept ourselves.

EXERCISE − Go to your space and make the decision to accept yourself—big butt, fat thighs, and all!

Part II

SECRETS TO SUCCESS: USING YOUR BIG BUTT

CONGRATULATIONS! YOU ARE ON YOUR WAY TO USING YOUR BIG butt as a tool to form invaluable relationships that will help you to achieve your career goals. Up until this point, you have unwittingly allowed your big butt to not only define you but also to sabotage your road to success. It is now time to take the energy you've wasted in protecting your vulnerabilities and reposition it to promote your strengths. You will learn, as I did, that your big butt, the albatross that has strangled your growth, may actuality be the key to unleashing your power.

Chapter Six shows you how to view yourself in terms of your professional identity and then induce others to perceive you in the same way. In Chapters Seven and Eight, you will learn the specific skills necessary to share your vulnerabilities and enable others to reciprocate, thereby building meaningful relationships. Chapter Nine shows you how to apply these principles with particularly challenging individuals. Finally, Chapter Ten encourages you to get off of your butt and go on to conquer your dreams!

Chapter Six

FROM PROTECTING YOUR BIG BUTT TO PROMOTING YOUR CAREER

IT IS NOW TIME TO STOP HIDING YOUR BIG BUTT AND INSTEAD start exposing your professional persona. It is important to note here that I am using the words *profession, job, business, career,* and *employment* in the loosest sense of the words. I'm speaking to your role as a pharmaceutical salesperson, web designer, corporate executive, physician, volunteer, or fund-raiser, to any vocation or avocation that you now participate in but yearn to excel in. I am also broadly using the words sell or promote to connote the ability to convince people to work with you, buy your products or services, agree with your ideas, invest in your nonprofits, fund your ventures, champion your causes, or support your advancement.

While I'm sure you will be familiar with some of the specific techniques for promoting your business, I believe it crucial to look at them through a new lens. They are your keys to refocusing your energy away from protecting your vulnerabilities and toward enhancing your professional identity.

Defining Yourself in Terms of Your Profession

My mother desperately tried to transform me from a child who was chubby and clumsy, to one who was slender and poised. To her credit, this is what she thought was in my best interest at the time, and she was determined not to give up. From summer camps to ballet lessons, she tried her best. She signed me up for the gamut of extracurricular activities including tap dancing and even cotillion. In spite of her good intentions, it was those previously mentioned baton lessons that helped jump start my true identity: not as an agile baton twirler, but as a burgeoning businesswoman.

With my new baton in hand, I attended weekly lessons. I was part of a group of about ten girls, standing in a circle as far apart as possible, as we wrestled with our shiny instruments. We learned how to transfer the baton from one hand to another, twirl it around our hands and throw it up high into the air, sometimes actually catching it before it hit the ground. I was not horrible at this, but could not really see the point, as I was never going to don one of those skimpy outfits with the fringe and march down the streets of Miami, in the Orange Bowl Parade. However, an idea started to develop.

After about the second or third lesson, I came home and rounded up the neighborhood girls. For twenty-five cents each, I offered to teach them what I had just learned. I was soon in business and had taken the first step to transforming my own image from a chubby, awkward misfit to an entrepreneur.

I continued the process of refocusing my identity when I sold those Girl Scout Cookies and discovered that I was an excellent salesperson. I liked making money and I loved experiencing success. I realized that if I believed in a product, I could sell it. Soon, I was going door-to-door selling greeting cards and later graduated to working in retail and eventually to more sophisticated entrepreneurial endeavors.

Without consciously realizing it, I had begun to think more about making the next sale, than what I looked like while making the next sale. For moments at a time, I forgot about my big butt. As my success grew, these moments stretched into days, weeks, and months. Soon, instead of *being* my big butt, I was a successful entrepreneur who just happened to *have* a big butt.

My identity as a businesswoman was not confined to the workplace; it permeated my existence. I talked about my business, read articles pertaining to my business, marketed my business, and dreamt about my business. How exhilarating to spend my mental resources going after my dreams rather than dwelling on my vulnerabilities. I also determined early on that I didn't want to be identified as simply a businesswoman; rather, I wanted to be known as an *excellent* businesswoman. To sell this image to myself and others I had to present myself with competence and confidence. I had to keep my word and at least meet, if not beat, expectations. I had to build trust and foster confidence in my colleagues and clients. It was imperative that I was forthright and reliable. I needed to be the go-to person in my industry.

Like me, your professional identity cannot merely be worn in the workplace, but must be integrated into your persona. There is a wide gap between knowing what you do and being what you do. For example, most of us can say the words, "I'm a broker," or "I'm an accountant," or "I'm head of the PTA." We can express what we do. However, to make a real impact on your career, your identification must be bigger than mere words. You must see and present yourself as a broker, an accountant, a top volunteer. An effective technique to begin bridging the gap, from knowing who you are to being who you are, is formulating a meaningful professional identity statement.

A professional identity statement is simply your personal description of what you do and what makes you special. What differentiates you from the crowd? Why should other people avail themselves of your products and services or fund your ideas or causes? What advantage will they gain by working with you? Are you extremely knowledgeable or experienced in your field? Are you willing to go the extra mile for a client? Do you have unique skills? Are you particularly fun to work with?

Elise was starting her own tutoring business, specializing in high school English. After spending so much of her time saddled with her big butt, a generalized fear that she was truly a failure and would not succeed in anything, she was stymied as to why prospective students or their parents would choose her. To help Elise differentiate herself and come up with a personal identity statement, I pointedly asked, "My neighbor's daughter has her final exam in French literature next month. What could you do to help her achieve a good grade?" Elise's passion trumped her insecurities, as she succinctly set forth the curriculum she would put my neighbor's daughter through to help her master the French authors. Fervently, she went on to tell me how she would work extra hours and do whatever it took to make sure this student succeeded. "Fabulous!" I responded. You now have your statement. As the light bulb went on, Elise was able to write, "I am an English tutor. I am well educated in all genres of literature. I am able to succinctly differentiate and elaborate on various writing styles, and most important, I can convey this in a manner that enables the student to comprehend and enjoy their readings. I will do whatever it takes to ensure their success." Elise had her statement. My neighbor had a tutor.

Once you have your statement, read it first thing in the morning and last thing in the evening. Commit it to memory. You are on your way to becoming your profession. Continue reinforcing this message when you are getting dressed for work in the morning. Standing in front of the mirror, focus your attention on how you will pitch this afternoon's sale, not on whether your skirt makes your hips look too big. On your commute to work, prepare for the day by reading or listening to pertinent professional materials, rather than a magazine article on how to achieve fuller lips. You will slowly begin to see yourself through a different lens— you are a successful professional. Your butt has not shrunk, your hips have not contracted; rather, you are no longer making them your focus. You are transferring the negative energy of your big butt obsession into the positive energy of promoting your professional goals.

Like any new skill, seeing yourself as a confident professional, rather than as someone with a big butt, takes patience, consistency, and practice. Until this becomes natural for you, just act "*as if.*" In other words, imagine how you would act if you were at the top of your game. To help you visualize this image think of how a specific supervisor or other role model presents herself. Before too long, you will no longer be acting as if you were a successful professional, you will be one. Do you remember the first time you tried on your graduation cap and gown? Remember that feeling of seeing yourself in a different light and swelling up with pride over your accomplishments? Similarly, think about the first time you tiptoed into a bridal store, tried on a gown and saw yourself as a bride? Looking at ourselves differently always takes that tentative first step. But, if you consistently remind yourself to wear the role, before long you won't even notice it is on.

I vividly remember my first courtroom appearance as a newly admitted member of the Bar. I felt like a complete fraud. What did I know about courtroom procedures? Who was I kidding? However, I played the role. I dressed the part and read the script. I obtained a favorable verdict, and the next court appearance was much easier. Soon, I was no longer playing— I was an attorney. I wore my identity everywhere I went from the courtroom, to the country club dining room. The contacts I made and the relationships I built with this identity proved invaluable as I transitioned into the business of law. The following tips will help you to cement your professional identity into your mind while you project an image of confidence and competence:

- Stand up tall and straight, head high and shoulders back.

- Meet people with a big smile and firm handshake.

- When you do not know someone, be proactive, and introduce yourself.

- When speaking to another person maintain direct eye contact.

- Ask yourself how you would act if you were a successful professional—then do it.

- Have your professional identity statement memorized, and look for opportunities to deliver it.

- Show passion about your work, it is contagious.

Promoting Your Professional Identity to Others

Once you see yourself in terms of your career, it is time to present and promote this identity to the outside world. It is my firm belief that nothing can help your career more than the ability to effectively promote yourself and your products, services, or interests. Whether you are a physician, an attorney, a software developer, or an accountant, you need to develop a following and bring in clients. If you're a researcher, an entrepreneur, or are involved in the nonprofit world – you must write grants and bring in funding. With few exceptions, regardless of your field, it is imperative that you see to it that your name is widely known and associated with excellence. This is absolutely necessary to help you rise to the top and become *the one* that people turn to for their purchases, services, investments, or philanthropy.

The benefits of widespread, effective self-promotion cannot be overemphasized. All things being equal, those individuals who can effectively promote themselves will be the most successful in bringing in revenue. This ability to bring in revenue will not only translate to financial success, it will also open the door to increased options and personal freedom. Rainmakers are highly sought after in the job market and often earn the luxury of control over their schedules and environment. Similarly, people who can raise money in nonprofit, political, or other organizations are revered. Like it or not, no matter how hard you work or how good you are, the ability to bring in business is still a highly coveted asset. The business will come by effectively promoting yourself so that as many people as possible know what you do and know that you do it consistently with precision, skill, and excellence. You cannot keep your talents a secret and expect to be successful; hence the billions of dollars spent in advertising and marketing.

Katherine is one of the most prominent real estate agents in her area. For many years, the fact that she was still single, her big butt, defined her. Her energy was consumed with trying to find a husband and, at the same time, making sure that she was not judged negatively for being single. To this end, her conversations were centered on men; either whining about the scarcity of prospects or explaining why it wasn't her fault her latest beau did not call her back. She relentlessly grilled her friends for names of eligible prospects and spent her free time pursuing singles venues instead of new clients. Now, well into middle age, rather than seeing herself as an old maid, she sees herself as a fabulous businesswoman.

Katherine had finally convinced herself that the right man would come along when it was meant to be, and rather than focusing on her big butt, she made the decision to redirect her energy into growing her budding business. Now, everyone who knows Katherine knows what she does. From efficiently using social media tools like Facebook and Twitter as well as old fashion business cards and seminars, Katherine has effectively marketed and defined herself as a real estate agent. She is now focusing her efforts on getting her broker's license and having other agents work for her. Yes, she would still love to find Mr. Right, but, she is happy and flourishing in her career.

Tara, a social worker, is the director of a small nonprofit for children with special needs. Like most nonprofit directors, her biggest challenge is raising sufficient funds to run the program. While comfortable in her social-worker role, she was very uneasy raising money. Her big butt, the fact that she thinks she is inadequate when playing with the boys, keeps her from aggressively going after potential donors. Tara had a rude awakening when she was informed by the chair of her board that there were rumblings amongst board members that they needed a director who would bring in more funding.

Tara and I had many long talks, and she finally agreed to quit paying attention to her big butt and, instead, start promoting her charity. She began with a personal identity statement. "I am the director of XYZ. We fulfill the essential needs of our children. Every dollar that we raise goes toward helping these precious kids. It is not an option—we simply cannot let them down—they depend on us. I hope they can also depend on you." With practice she became more comfortable soliciting funding. She also realized that her efforts could not be confined to work-related situations. She needed to make her interests known wherever she went and with whomever she came into contact. The more she pitched her cause, the more comfortable she became. This year was a record-breaking year for donations, and Tara is energized and excited. "I didn't think that I could attract donors in nontraditional venues like my hair salon," she observed. "The key for me was to get our name out. Our mission is inherently compelling—but, I needed to transition my energy into publicizing it to as many different people as possible."

To maximize the effects of your professional efforts it is essential to follow Katherine and Tara's examples and begin by defining yourself in terms of your career—both in and out of the workplace. Once you're able to see yourself in this light, the following practices will help you to promote your professional persona to the outside world.

1. Wear Your Business Identity on Your Sleeve

Do not leave your business identity at work— take it with you wherever you go. You never know where the next client will come from. Instead of trying to hide yourself, so people won't notice your big butt, reveal yourself so people will notice your profession. View every person and every situation, and I mean every person and every situation, as a potential opportunity to meet new clients. I'm talking about waiters, librarians, soccer moms, fellow passengers, and physicians. I'm referring to situations from cocktail parties to back-to-school nights, from the gym to the bookstore. By wearing your identity on your sleeve and exposing it to as many people as possible, you will promote yourself and increase your contact base. I will explain later, how to turn these contacts into relationships and eventually into clients.

It kills me when I see women so preoccupied with their big butts, that they miss crucial opportunities to promote their professional identity and connect with influential sources. I clearly remember going to a cocktail party with my friend Charlotte, a banker, whose big butt she describes as her "tree trunk" legs. She usually wears pants, but felt a dress was more appropriate for this particular venue. Exposing her legs made her exceptionally self-conscious as her big butt grew to gargantuan proportions in her mind. We ran into a mutual acquaintance who happened to be involved with real estate development and was looking for financing options. As he discussed his needs, I looked to my friend Charlotte— nothing. Surreptitiously, I kicked her—nothing.

Finally, no longer able to contain myself I asked her to accompany me to the ladies room. "Charlotte", I exclaimed. "Here is a great opportunity, why aren't you pursuing it? Let him know that you're a banker and can help him procure competitive financing." Thankfully, she agreed to forget about her legs for a moment and assume her professional identity; setting up an appointment with this potential client.

Charlotte is not alone in failing to make her professional identity known. Not too long ago, I was at the airport and could not help overhearing a woman talking to her supervisor about their health-care consulting business. Later, boarding the plane, this same woman sat across from me, and sitting next to her was someone obviously involved in the medical profession, as I could easily ascertain from his reading material. Curious, I was vigilant in observing my airport woman to see how she would divulge her identity as a health-care consultant. Nothing – she never even tried to initiate any kind of conversation. Another lost opportunity.

I implore you to start today. Wear your professional identity where everyone can easily see it. Since most of us do not wear a uniform broadcasting what we do for a living, it is necessary for us to sharpen our communication skills to convey our professional identity. Here are some effective ways to do this:

- Carry a stack of business cards and freely hand them out anywhere you can without coming off as tacky. Even when you transfer from a brief case to a tiny evening bag, in goes lipstick, cell phone, and business cards.

- Listen carefully, and vigilantly seek opportunities to let people know what you do.

- Ask others about what they do in order to open the door for work conversation.

- Have a funny story prepared to help you seamlessly introduce your work into conversations.

- Comment on current events, movies, or articles that apply to your area of expertise.

- Wear your business persona wherever you go.

2. See and be Seen

It is in your best interests to expose your professional identity to as many different people as possible. There is a direct correlation between the number of people who know what you do—and the number of people who will think of you when they have a need for your services. It follows that you must widen your net of visibility to meet potential clients and referral sources. There are many ways to expand your horizons. Take a leadership role in your community or industry. Get involved with interests you are passionate about; from nonprofit boards to book clubs, exposure is the key. Join effective leads groups, women's groups and other groups specifically focused on client development. Or, like my friend Martha, create your own networking group. She hand selected a group of twenty high- powered women from diverse industries who meet on a monthly basis to help and promote one another.

Another effective way to be seen is to attend events that attract large and powerful crowds. While industry events and company gatherings attract industry specific attendees, other events, though not specifically geared toward your niche, may prove to be equally rewarding for networking purposes. Functions such as political fund-raisers and charity galas are great for attracting movers and shakers with vast networks of friends and colleagues to share with you.

Now that your big butt no longer keeps you hidden away, try attending a variety of different events to find those most worthwhile for your particular goals. You want to maintain an open, approachable presence and mingle with a wide array of people. You no longer have anything to hide—you now have something to say. You want to promote your business identity. A word of caution, if you ask a girlfriend to go with you, separate once you get there. Do not walk around the room like two ducklings, attached at the hip. This does not convey competence and makes it more difficult for others to approach you. You will find that the more events you attend, the more people you will know. And like anything else, practice makes perfect. The more you go out the more comfortable you will become. Here are some useful strategies:

- Have a few icebreakers ready to initiate conversations.

- Have your business cards easily accessible.

- Do not sit in a corner— you are there to meet and mingle.

- Introduce yourself, or ask a third party to introduce you to people you want to meet. Reciprocate, and offer to make introductions for others.

- Try to be helpful to other attendees, know where the bar and restrooms are located.

- Ask for the other person's card and write notes on the back to help you remember their needs and how you met them.

- Follow up. A quick email, a carefully structured note, or a shared article that pertains to their interests, are all effective techniques to keep your name in their minds.

- Use a database management system or other method to track your contacts, record important facts about them, and remind you when to reconnect with them.

- Either on the spot, or as soon after as possible, set up a face-to-face appointment with your new contact.

- Don't forget, your goal is to ask for business!

3. Be Informed

To bolster your professional identity you must ensure that you are knowledgeable about your industry, your competition, basic business principles, and current events. I am not saying that you have to be an economics professor, or an expert on foreign policy; what I am saying is you must have intricate knowledge about your industry and a basic understanding of factors that will influence your clients' decisions.

By staying on top of current trends, you can gingerly manipulate conversations to give yourself the opportunity to share your knowledge in a constructive manner. In this way, you are bolstering your professional identity by encouraging potential clients to rely on your expertise. Sara, a web designer, was a master at bringing up her technology skills to the right people in the right situations. Previously encumbered with a slight learning disability, her big butt, she successfully rechanneled her energy into promoting her business. I was on the treadmill at the gym to the right of Sara, when I overheard her talking to the women on her left. "I went on your website yesterday," Sara shared. "I think it looks great, but I can't help but wonder whether you are taking advantage of the newest search engine maximization strategies." As they continued treading, Sara shared some of the newest trends. At the end, sweaty and successful, Sara had a new client.

Like Sara, Jenny, an industrial psychologist, conscientiously kept herself informed. Downloading the morning paper on her iPad, she read an article about a national chain that was relocating into her area. Armed with this knowledge, and knowing that she was well equipped to assist employees with the stress associated with relocation, she called the head of human resources and set up a meeting to discuss their upcoming needs. By staying up to date on the news, she positioned herself to land a huge account.

Gina, on the other hand, lost a potential sale because she neglected to learn about basic business principles. She sold office furniture and was quite knowledgeable about the construction of desks and the numerous features of her vast inventory of chairs. However, she had no basic concept of business principles. Visiting a potential client, she asked, "How's business going?"

He replied, "Volume is holding its own, but margins are way down."

"Well that's great that volume is steady," she cheerfully replied.

"Don't you get it," he angrily retorted, we are making way less money and are having difficulty keeping our head above water."

Gina had no idea what he meant by margins. Her ignorance diminished her presence and she lost a customer.

The following tips will help to ensure that you present yourself as current and knowledgeable:

- Read, or at least skim a daily national paper like *The Wall Street Journal*, *The New York Times,* or *The Washington Post* as well as your local paper.

- Get a book on very basic business principles so that you're familiar with concepts such as net profit and gross margins.

- Become an expert on your industry, read trade journals and anything else you can get your hands on.

- Educate yourself on your clients' businesses.

4. Broadcast Your Expertise

You do not always have to be physically present to make your presence known. Look for any opportunities to demonstrate your expertise. You can market yourself as an expert in your field in numerous ways, including speaking engagements and publishing articles. My friend, Felicia, is a great example of a savvy personal marketer.

Felicia was a brilliant attorney, but she allowed her big butt to rule her. She had spent much of her life immersed in books and was extremely shy and self-conscious when interacting with others. The turning point for Felicia was when she was advised that to make partner at her firm it was important that she begin to develop new business. Out of desperation, Felicia agreed to try rechanneling her energy away from her insecurities and into promoting her expertise. She began by writing articles for trade magazines. She continued growing her reputation by speaking at seminars to potential, and eventually, actual clients. The more her status grew, the less her big butt mattered. Before she even realized it— she was responsible for a large book of business and was the go-to person in her field. Yes, eventually she even made partner. You can begin promoting your professional identity and showcasing your expertise by:

- Writing articles for newspapers, periodicals and trade journals

- Using social media

- Creating a blog and contributing to others' blogs

- Creating seminars and focus groups

- Teaching

- Coming up with a clever angle for radio or television

- Pitching stories for print media

- Booking speaking engagements

5. Refer to Get Referrals

Whether we're looking for a consultant or a mechanic, we ask those we trust for referrals. When multiple sources recommend the same person or company, our confidence increases and we will almost always take the referral. Come to think of it, it is ironic that we really don't know if the referral is the best in her industry. All we know is that she has been able to effectively promote herself so that her name is the one that comes to people's minds when they are asked for a referral. Better consultants or mechanics may exist, but without marketing or promoting themselves, they excel in isolation. In other words, if we look at two equally skilled consultants, the one whose name is better recognized will be the one to attract more clients.

Clearly, it is in your best interest to successfully promote your identity so that your name is in the forefront of people's minds when they are asked for a referral. Inga, a geriatric consultant, is very involved with her religious organization. She attends as many functions as possible and possesses a confident and likeable demeanor. Her name has become synonymous with geriatric care. I think half of the organization has used her services for themselves or their parents!

Inga understands that referring business to others is a terrific way to promote your own professional identity. As the old adage states, "What goes around comes around." Referrals beget referrals. Create a circle of service providers that you respect and are comfortable referring. Make sure, that when you pass their name on to someone else, you say something like, "Please let Charlotte know that I gave you her name. I'm sure she will take great care of you." Over time, these people should refer back to you, and if not, you may want to consider whether you know someone else equally competent. When you make a referral it is a reflection on you, so make sure that you are comfortable with the person's abilities. Again, you have no way of discerning if that person is the best in their field, but you can detect if they are solid and competent.

When someone is referred to you, take the highest degree of care with that person. You want to maintain your reputation for excellence, and you want to ensure there will be other referrals to follow. Most important, thank the referrer immediately. A sincere phone call or handwritten note will remind them to keep you foremost in their mind.

How great it feels to harness all that energy you wasted in trying to protect your big butt and instead redirect it in a positive manner to promoting your business. As we've seen, before you can convince others of your professional value, you must first convince yourself. Your conviction will help you present yourself with competence and confidence. This confidence will shine through in your communications and body language. Pair this growing confidence with passion, and it becomes irresistible to others.

Promoting your career is only the beginning. You must then continue to keep your name alive and build up your cadre of contacts. In the following chapters we will see how, by using our big butts, we can develop these contacts into the kinds of relationships that will eventually lead to business.

Chapter Seven

SHARING IMPERFECTIONS:
I'LL SHOW YOU MINE

LET'S MAKE SURE THAT THERE ARE NO MISUNDERSTANDINGS — you are still not perfect. You have not gotten rid of your big butt, or, for most of us, big *butts*. There are still parts of yourself that you would prefer to get rid of. What you have done is accepted your flaws and refused to allow them to define you. You see that they are merely a part of you —but that you are so much more. You have taken all of that mental energy away from the things you could not control and have now redirected it into those you can: your professional identity, goals, and career path.

The next step is perhaps the simplest. You are now required to simply be your real self while simultaneously promoting your professional identity. It's very important to understand that your *professional persona* and your *real self* are not mutually exclusive concepts. Too many of us mistakenly equate being professional with being stiff, starched, dispassionate, and unreal. Granted, many professions and situations certainly call for appropriate dress and decorum. That being said, you can abide by such protocols while still maintaining your authenticity.

The ability to advance your professional goals while maintaining your authenticity is an invaluable skill that differentiates the rainmakers from the rest of the pack. Most people can walk into another's office, find out that they both play golf, and form a *connection*. Your goal is to walk into another's office, find out that you both hate how you look in golf shorts, and form a *bond.*

Your real self is what attracts others to you and motivates them to want to form deeper and more meaningful relationships. The key to establishing genuine, useful, and long-lasting bonds with others is to share your vulnerabilities, while at the same time creating a comfortable atmosphere that makes others want to share their vulnerabilities with you.

In the process of identifying your own big butt, you came to realize that everyone has one. The way they deal with it can manifest itself in a myriad of different behaviors. But, everyone wastes, as you did, tremendous time and energy trying to shelter their big butts from exposure. Everyone feels, as you did, that their big butts are a sign of inadequacy. No one wants to feel inadequate. By applying the insights you have gained in understanding the negative impact of your own big butt on your life, you can now effectively understand and empathize with the plights of others. A networking encounter I had with Yvonne, head of human resources of a well-known company, serves to poignantly demonstrate the benefits of sharing vulnerabilities within a professional context.

It was one of those quaint, local coffee shops. I was meeting Yvonne at 9 a.m. A friend of mine arranged the meeting because she thought Yvonne and I should meet one another, as we had a lot in common and could help each other's careers.

I arrived a few minutes early, claiming a table in the corner so that we could talk in private. I sat facing the door, watching for Yvonne. She was prompt and exuded a sophisticated air when she came in. She had a stylish haircut and wore beautifully tailored pants with a cashmere sweater. Her jewelry, which perfectly accented her outfit, was carefully selected to be appropriate but not ostentatious.

Initially, we exchanged small talk. I asked her to tell me about herself. Where was she from? How did she get to this place in her life? She recited a cursory summation of her achievements and education. Cautiously avoiding anything personal, she stuck with resume facts.

I patiently listened to her shallow narration, asking questions where appropriate. To be polite, she reciprocated, and asked me to convey my story. At this point, I could have easily chosen to follow her lead and not reveal anything personal. I could have given her a factual account of my career, sticking to the usual script. If I had chosen this path, our meeting would have quickly wrapped up. We would have left the café as social acquaintances. A more satisfying and rewarding relationship would have been thwarted. Instead, I chose to share some of my real self. She was particularly interested in hearing about how we started and grew our company. Rather than glossing over the obstacles, I made a concerted decision to reveal some of the messy and unabridged truth.

"My partner and I had just rented a small office on the fifth floor of an old building in downtown Baltimore," I began. "Our staff was just the two of us. We answered the phones, read the mail and began the process of marketing our services. We were scared, but mostly excited. We loved the idea of owning our own business and were both relieved to stop practicing law." I paused, took a deep breath and plunged in, "Everything was running pretty smoothly, until one hot and humid summer night, when my marriage of fifteen years came to an end."

Recalling the exact moment my marriage was over, I shared with Yvonne, "I felt like the floor had opened, and I was falling into a dark and deep pit. My children were young. Our business was brand new. I didn't know how I was going to survive through the night, no less the rest of my life."

From Yvonne's concerned and interested expression, I knew it was OK to go on. "The next morning, I walked into our office and told my partner what had happened, that I was getting divorced. He looked at me with sympathetic eyes and asked, 'Do you want to close the office and go back to practicing law?'

"'No!' I told him. From somewhere deep inside, I knew with certainty that we were going to build a successful business. From that moment on, failure was never an option."

Yvonne seemed to be genuinely moved by my story. When I finished, she looked directly in my eyes with a new level of understanding. Now, it was her turn.

She began to revise the previous, perfunctory summary of her life; it was now punctuated with stories of her own challenges, hurts, and vulnerabilities. It turned out that her youngest daughter was a recovering alcoholic. Her mother was fighting a devastating illness, and her father had recently passed away.

I looked at her again. I really looked at her. This professional, impeccably dressed woman had not only risen to high levels of professional achievement but had done so in the face of real challenges. I now not only respected her, I truly admired her.

We left our cozy booth with our coffee cups empty; our relationship, full. In the ensuing years, I was able to motivate Yvonne to reach new goals. In turn, with her network of contacts, she was able to help me open some tightly closed doors to influential decision makers. I had taken the chance and shown her a piece of my real self. This set the tone, and allowed her to reciprocate. We each only revealed what we were comfortable sharing. It was enough to enable us to form a lasting bond based on authenticity and trust.

Women Connect Naturally by Sharing Vulnerabilities

In our friendships with other women, we naturally connect to one another by sharing our vulnerabilities. How many hours have you spent discussing with friends your issues concerning men, mothers, children, weight, wrinkles, and other such topics? The closer the friendship, the more deeply we delve. We crave permission to process our feelings. We covet the opportunity to be validated. In this process, we become alive. How liberating to be ourselves, absent any pretense. We treasure those who allow us to just be, those who do not demand that we work for validation. We do not have to put on makeup, sport special labels, or even clean our house before they visit. They love and accept us just because we are who we are.

Now that you have made peace with your big butt, you can drop the heavy burden of protecting it and just be your real self. Not only do you no longer need to hide it, but you can actually expose it and in this way set the tone for relaxed, comfortable conversation. There is nothing that allows another person to feel more comfortable with you than when you are comfortable enough to accept and expose your own flaws.

Even when we understand the benefits of sharing our big butts, it is not always easy to do so in the workplace. We fear that if we expose any vulnerability, we will be judged and disliked or disrespected. "They" will see us as incompetent, neurotic, or insecure. We bear such an unnecessary burden by our mistaken belief that showing any imperfections will undermine our professional credentials. On the contrary, our work product speaks for itself. It is actually, by *not* sharing any of who we truly are, by not being authentic, that we hinder our careers. If we fail to be authentic we fail to make real connections—the kind of connections that bring us professional success.

Just to be perfectly clear, I am not saying to be inappropriate. I am not telling you to let it all hang out and walk in naked to your next business meeting. What I am saying is that it's OK if your butt looks big in appropriate business attire. The following guidelines will help you learn how and when to share your big butt in an appropriate manner.

The Sooner You Learn How to Reveal Your Big Butt, the Better

Like any new behavior, the sooner we start learning to change, the easier it becomes. As you start "showing yours" by being genuine and revealing some of yourself, you will set the tone for others to "show you theirs." The more you practice, the more skilled you will become in this carefully choreographed dance. As with all newly learned behaviors, when you start receiving positive feedback, your behavior will be reinforced and, over time, lead to a new, easy and genuine way of relating.

On the other hand, the longer we go without revealing any vulnerability, staying isolated in our self-built fortresses, the harder it is for us to break free. We retreat further and further from our true selves, trying to protect our big butts. We forget who we really are behind the mask. Sometimes, we become the mask.

Begin with Easy Icebreakers

As with any new skill or behavior, the first step is the most difficult. Women often ask, "How do I begin? Tell me exactly what to say." After too many years of conditioning in hiding our real selves, we may find it hard to break the cycle. It helps to draw on the knowledge discussed in the prior chapters that you are not alone. Everyone has a big butt. And remember, this is a strategic decision to enrich your work relationships by sharing your vulnerabilities. You are not necessarily trying to make business associates your best friends; you just want to connect on a genuine level.

You only have to reveal as much as you are comfortable revealing. As most of us have many big butts, start with the easy ones. We do not need to start by sharing our biggest butt— depending on what it is, this may never be appropriate. Instead, we can begin by sharing *some* of our big butts. Here are a few sample icebreakers to get you started:

- I hate this rain; my hair can't handle the humidity.

- My son drives me nuts, I told him to call as soon as he reached his destination, but so far, nothing.

- I always feel a little jittery waiting to speak.

- This bag is killing my shoulder.

- Men—sometimes I think they live on their own planet. Last night my husband sat and watched, as I cleaned up the entire kitchen.

- I know I should take more advantage of social networking sites to market my business, but I just don't know how to get started.

- It is so hard to get myself to the gym before work. I know I should, but I'd rather roll over and go back to sleep.

Think of Company Picnics and Retreats

You have probably already been in a situation where you were forced to get outside of your business persona. Do you remember your first company picnic? Or, the first time you were with your co-workers or clients outside of the office, in a different context? One of my first experiences was in the worst possible place—the beach.

As providers of legal services, we needed to attend the Annual State Bar Convention. We were to exhibit at the show and network with attorneys throughout the state. Much to my chagrin, the convention was always held during the summer on the Maryland coast. Just the thought of going to the beach with colleagues thrust me way out of my comfort zone. As a lawyer, I was always protected with navy blue, black, or gray business attire. I knew this role, and was very uncomfortable diverting from the safe, conservative dress. Now, was I going to parade around in a bathing suit? No way!

The first year we attended, the furthest I could push myself was to khakis and a white tee shirt. I could not possibly consider exposing any more. The following year, at the same convention, I actually progressed to shorts. Eventually, many years later, I could walk on the beach with a bathing suit and cover-up!

This slow peeling of layers of clothing is a fitting metaphor for the peeling of the layers of defensive attire protecting your vulnerabilities. You are already getting out of your role when you attend work-related picnics, retreats, and sporting events. Think about taking off your business suit, as you try to shed some of your other protective armor. This does not mean telling all, just as it does not mean parading around in a thong. Just let some of who you really are show through. Remember, you are not alone in your discomfort. Think of the long lines at the bar, when you attend most of these off-site work events!

Admit Mistakes or that You Do not Have all the Answers

There is nothing more human than making a mistake. Admitting our mistakes is a natural way to share our big butts. For some reason, we are terrified of making any type of error and obsess over details to ensure perfection. This need for perfection often paralyzes us from making decisions and taking action. When we do make a mistake, we take it personally and allow it to wound our already fragile egos; or, alternatively, we become defensive and avoid taking responsibility for the gaffe.

By simply admitting our mistakes and moving on, we exhibit strength of character. We have not changed; we are still the preeminent professional. We are also human and occasionally mess up. We allow those who work with us to relax in our presence, knowing perfection is not required at all times.

Sharon, a woman I greatly respect, taught me this lesson. She was brilliant and hugely successful, yet every once in a while, like all of us, she made a mistake. The first time it happened she said, "Whoops! You won't believe what I just did." By these simple words, Sharon set the stage, so that no one around her had to shiver and walk on egg shells to avoid the inevitable slipup.

Then there was Nancy. She was in charge of a large and stressful project. She needed to devise a marketing plan for recruitment. To this end, an advertisement was to be placed in Sunday's newspaper, so that eligible candidates could apply the following Monday. The newspaper's deadline was 3 p.m. on Friday. Nancy got tied up on a conference call and missed the deadline. She came straight into my office, looked into my eyes, and accepted full responsibility.

"I am so sorry, I really messed up. I missed the deadline." She went on to tell me how this happened, and what she would try to do to minimize damages. I knew she was distraught, but in my eyes, she gained my respect. She took responsibility and was not defensive. She went on to become one of our superstars. Ninety-nine percent of her work was great. She was simply human. Mistakes happen.

Just like admitting our mistakes, saying "I don't know" is a way of sharing our vulnerabilities. How many times have you prepared for a meeting or presentation and thought you had gathered every piece of relevant information? Unexpectedly, someone throws out a question and you simply do not know the answer. This is a perfect opportunity to show your big butt and move on.

Too often, caught in this situation, we either become defensive or obsessively berate ourselves for not knowing. "Nobody told me to look into those statistics!" Katherine protectively lashed out, when asked something she did not know. "How was I supposed to know to check into that?" she continued.

In a similar and just as destructive tactic, Annabelle, when asked a question for which she did not have an answer, whined, "I am so sorry. I can't believe I am that stupid." She pitifully continued, "I tried so hard. I should have known to look into that." Even worse, she continued for much too long to chastise herself and obsess over her gaffe.

A simple, "I don't know, but I will find out" is all it takes to show your vulnerability, and keep your professionalism intact.

We can all relate to someone's humanness in not knowing. We have all been in similar situations. On the other hand, the defensive or the "feel sorry for me" tactic diminishes your professionalism and discourages connections.

Only Reveal What Is Appropriately Comfortable

We want to show that we are human and approachable. We want to set the stage for others to be comfortable in our presence. We do not want to cross the line and appear as complete messes. Remember, the key is to show that we are strong and competent, but not perfect. I am often asked how much should I reveal? What is too much? This is best answered on a case-by-case basis, but in general:

- Never reveal anything personal about someone else.

- Start slowly—give the relationship time to naturally develop.

- Make sure you are sharing with someone you can trust.

- Do not share much more than you receive.

- Stay attuned to the other person's reaction to your disclosures and react accordingly.

- Ask yourself, if the vulnerability you share reaches the ears of other people, could it cause you detrimental consequences?

The focus of your encounters is to help achieve your business and professional goals. Self-revelations serve to set the stage to form real relationships. You are not revealing so much as to appear weird or make the other person uncomfortable. Start slowly and gauge the other person's reaction. Appropriately sharing your big butt is an art not a science. By practicing and experimenting you will learn how and where to draw the line. Avoid, as my children say, "TMI—too much information!"

EXERCISE – This month, using the above principles, look for opportunities to share your big butt. Keep a notebook to keep track of the responses. Specifically, target two people with whom you would like to form an important connection, and share a little of your vulnerabilities with them.

Chapter Eight

NOW YOU SHOW ME YOURS

I KNOW THE EXACT MOMENT MY HUSBAND FELL DEEPLY AND unconditionally in love with me. It was the first time we slept together. No, it was not because of my sexual prowess. It was because I validated his biggest vulnerability. No, it's not what you are thinking —it was his sleep apnea machine.

Yes, the atmosphere was charged with energy and anticipation. However, having gone through a divorce, my ego was fragile. I was coping with recent rejection and saddled with my big butt, fat thighs and other miscellaneous cosmetic don'ts. So, while he was in the bathroom, I turned off all the lights and with unprecedented speed and agility, I dove under the covers. Between the darkness of the room and the shield of the blankets, I began to settle down.

Trying to remain calm, I kept glancing at the door waiting for his entrance. He finally walked in carrying a small black suitcase. "This is odd," I thought to myself. I did not think men brought overnight cases. Sheepishly, he looked at me and said, "Where is the closest outlet?" I looked at him questioningly as he went on to explain, "I need to plug in my CPAP machine."

To be fair, I was warned, but I was definitely not prepared. When it was time to go to sleep, he reached over and covered his face with what looked like a Darth-Vader-type oxygen mask one might use when entering a toxic waste site. It had a long, clear, plastic hose that connected the mask to his machine. Feeling his intense embarrassment, I was able to refrain from hysterical laughter. I did not minimize the event, just tried to be accepting and loving. It worked. This was not a one-way acceptance. He accepted my big butt and my myriad of other flaws. Embracing one another's vulnerabilities formed an indestructible connection. We were engaged shortly thereafter.

This bedroom story offers an important lesson for the boardroom. We must be open to and respect the vulnerabilities of others when they share themselves with us. When we reveal our big butts to them, they may reciprocate, or, they may need a little help from us to enable them to open up. Either way it is important to know how to both encourage and support their openness. The following principles will help you to allow another person to reveal their own big butts.

Listen and Observe

Some of our flaws are self-evident. We can easily see someone's big butt, large ears, pimply face, or frizzy hair. Other vulnerabilities are beneath the surface and only visible to their owners. By carefully listening and observing what they say and sometimes, more important, what they do not say, you can figure out the other person's Achilles' heel. You do not want to make them uncomfortable, or put them in a position of revealing what they choose not to disclose. You can, however, be attuned and sensitive, encouraging them to relax and be themselves.

I was at a party and Evelyn, a hedge fund manager, was behind me in line at the bar. She had always worn a thick coat of armor, shielding her real self from public view. I had been intrigued by her intelligence and keen decision-making skills, but felt I did not have any clue as to the real Evelyn. I took the opportunity, in this casual venue, to reach out and make a personal connection.

"So, tell me what you do exactly. I know you are a hedge fund manager, but what does that really mean?" I gently began.

"I manage various financial instruments," she vaguely replied.

"This must be a challenging economic environment for you," I carefully probed.

She replied with some sort of vague answer, and I tip-toed on. "I've always been intrigued when someone says they manage funds, but I do not have a real feel of what it is like. Could you give me a typical day, so that I can have a better understanding?"

We went on to talk for a good thirty minutes or more. She not only opened up about her job, but confessed her fear for the future security of her position, her big butt. She discussed possible upcoming opportunities and we talked about the pros and cons of each. When it became evident that we were being rude and ignoring others, we decided to continue over lunch at a later date. We both wanted to pursue a stronger connection, and knew that we could be assets to one another in our respective fields. Her final remarks succinctly summed up our conversation.

"I never reveal myself to anyone," she observed. "I can't believe I told you so much. It was a pleasure and I look forward to seeing you again, soon." By carefully listening and asking the right questions, I was able to help Evelyn let down her guard, reveal some of her big butt and really talk to me.

Appreciate, Reinforce, and Validate

Once you've made the commitment to be yourself and quit trying to hide your own big butt, you can appreciate the courage it takes for someone else to share a piece of their true self with you. When someone reveals her vulnerabilities, it is a gift that you must guard and respect. Most people in the workplace carefully cover up their real selves. If someone trusts you enough to reveal a part of herself that she is not thrilled with, or may be embarrassed by, you need to respond in an appropriate manner.

Sometimes, our tendency is either to ignore the person's revelation, or to diminish it to protect our own discomfort in witnessing the other person's unease. I remember when one of our managers, Maria, who was very overweight, confessed to a co-worker, Kelly, that she hated herself because of her weight. It made her self-conscious and miserable. Kelly felt uncomfortable hearing of Maria's distress, so she minimized it by replying, "Oh, you're not that heavy." Kelly went on to quickly change the subject because she was embarrassed for Maria and did not know how to respond.

Maria would have been much more satisfied and connected if Kelly had acknowledged and reinforced her confession, rather than dismissing it. For example, Kelly could have responded by saying, "I can't imagine how hard it must be for you. Is there anything I can do to make things easier in the office?" In this way, Kelly would have validated Maria's feelings. By offering to help, she would have shown kindness and made a connection. Kelly could have further reinforced Maria's revelation by disclosing some of her own big butt.

The old adage goes, "Surgery is only minor when someone else is having it." The same principles apply to our big butts. Whatever our insecurities, and however trivial they may seem to others, they are real and troublesome to us. It is never helpful when someone else minimizes them or shows us how someone else is in worse shape. As women, we seize the opportunity to process information and simply vent in a safe environment. In return, we want a trusting and non-judgmental response.

Be Safe and Trustworthy

We will not share our big butts with someone we do not trust. We want our secrets to stay with that person. No one wants to be talked about or be the subject for the latest water cooler gossip. Oftentimes people will test your ability to keep their information private, by giving you small kernels to digest. Treasure these, and keep them with you. You only have one reputation, and cannot buy or easily develop a new one. Make sure you meet the highest levels of trust and character.

Beth is a player in the world of high fashion. She is fun loving, with a zest for life. Her enthusiasm and energy attract many friends and business connections. Unfortunately, once you engage Beth in conversation, you quickly find out that she is the center of the gossip mill. "I trust you not to tell anybody this, but did you know that Harriet is thinking of leaving her job?" she reports to me. The tidbits of gossip are recklessly tossed out, with a careless disregard for where they might fall.

There is no way I would divulge my real vulnerabilities to Beth. Most of her relationships are poorly developed and superficial. Yes, she is fun, but her loose lips prevent her from forming the kind of connections that will genuinely serve to further her business goals. We must provide a safe environment, to enable others to share what really matters most to them.

A safe environment is also created by complimenting others on their strengths and overlooking their weaknesses. Women consumed with protecting their liabilities are desperate for confirmation of their assets. When you readily and sincerely validate those attributes in someone else that they are proud of, you make it easier for them to share those things they are ashamed of. By becoming proactive in recognizing the strengths of others, you will create an environment conducive to trust.

Likewise, as we already feel bad enough about our big butts, it is almost always counterproductive to put us in the position of defending our actions or omissions. Once we have to justify ourselves, we are likely to retreat and will not risk exposing any additional shortcomings. While criticism is occasionally unavoidable, it is in your best interest to keep it to a minimum and to create a safe, validating environment.

Once you have sharpened your skills, it's time for a real challenge: interacting with people who do not want to see your big butt and absolutely do not want to show you theirs. Read on.

EXERCISE – This month observe the people in your work life and try to be aware of their vulnerabilities. Keep a notebook to record your discoveries. Find someone with whom you would like to develop a stronger business connection and try to help them open up to you.

Chapter Nine

SHARING WITH MEN AND OTHER SEEMINGLY EMOTIONLESS BEINGS

ONE NIGHT, MY HUSBAND, CHARLES, WENT OUT FOR DRINKS WITH a couple of guys. I knew that one of the guys, Doug, was involved with some very messy personal matters because his wife had opened up to me about them. I was naturally curious to find out Doug's take on the situation. When Charles finally came home, I immediately grilled him. "So, what did Doug say? How is he doing? Do you think they will be able to resolve this?"

Charles looked at me as if I were speaking a foreign language. "What are you talking about—it never came up. Guys don't talk about that kind of stuff," he retorted.

"Come on," I insisted. "You've got to be kidding! How could you *not* talk about it? What *did* you talk about?" I asked in an unbelieving voice.

Already tired of this line of questioning he shrugged, "Nothing, really."

One last try, "You had to talk about *something*!"

He thought for a second and finally came clean, "The food, the drinks, and we watched the game."

Even if They Won't Admit it—Men Have Big Butts Too

As this scenario demonstrates, men may be even less willing than us to expose their big butts. It's not that they don't have big butts—they have plenty of both physical and intangible inadequacies. Like us, men fret over their perceived physical flaws. From balding heads to pot bellies; hairy chests to hairless chests; miniscule pectorals to other small appendages—men have big butts.

On the intangible side, men have feelings of inadequacy over everything from their ability to adequately provide to their ability to adequately perform. They agonize over their athletic prowess and their social competence. Their insecurities may be compounded by their sense of competitiveness. They'll "show you theirs" all right, but only if what they're showing gives them bragging rights.

So, it's not that men do not have big butts—it's just that they are not as motivated or willing to share them. They fall victim to the implicit societal taboo discouraging the expression of such feelings. While as women, we naturally connect through our vulnerabilities—men play "whose is bigger." And this contest seems to include everything from car engines to flat screens and beyond.

I will admit that I am speaking in stereotypical generalities. There are indeed men who do not compete and men who are more than willing to openly discuss their insecurities and vulnerabilities. There are even some men who are more willing to share their big butts than their female counterparts.

This being said, I am now specifically addressing those men, and later, those women, who not only dread exposing their big butts, but would rather be hung by their fingernails than voluntarily bring up their shortcomings. So, how do we break through? How do we use our big butts to make important and lasting connections with men? We can start by communicating with them in a nonthreatening manner, encouraging them to drop their guard, relax, and maybe even share. Let me give you an example.

One day, I was sitting across the mammoth, mahogany desk, of the litigation partner of a prestigious northeast law firm, scanning his office for something I could use to break the ice. Most of the office was cluttered with "man trophies"—a huge mounted buck's head and numerous fishing paraphernalia. "This is going to be challenging," I thought. Continuing my quest, I spotted a picture of three smiling children. Before I even had a chance to comment, he looked at his watch, and indicated that I was infringing on his time. Sharply, he asked, "What can I do for you?"

Relying on a hunch, I looked toward the picture, smiled and ventured forward, "I'll just take a few minutes of your time. But, I can't help noticing your beautiful children, if you don't mind me asking, how old are they?" His body language quickly changed as a wretched look swept over his face. Maintaining direct eye contact, I leaned forward and gave a slight nod to nudge him on.

He clearly felt he was safe, and was being encouraged to elaborate. "I am recently separated," he sighed. "I just feel so bad for my kids."

At this time, my own divorce was still an open wound. I responded to his trusting self-revelation and shared some of my own pain. "It's awful, isn't it? I never expected that I would be in this position at this stage of my life." Being careful not to say too much or push too hard, I paused and subtly urged him to continue. He did.

"It's been a bitter separation. My wife is bad mouthing me to my kids. They all hate me—I love my children. I know that I'm not blameless, but neither is she. My kids refuse to speak to me—I miss them terribly."

Through this exchange of confidences we formed a meaningful connection. He became a valued client. Through the years we continued to commiserate with one another while building a mutually rewarding business relationship.

Unfortunately, it is unrealistic to expect all men to share their big butts in the same way as this particular litigator. Many men have not even acknowledged their big butt to themselves—much less to someone else. Not unlike some of our women, many men have hidden their imperfections for so long that they are not even aware of what it is that they are protecting. And even if they were, they are about as likely to talk about their fear of failure as they are to describe their receding hair line. At least women seem to have an inner curiosity that motivates them to identify what it is that is holding them back. Men, often adhere to the old adage, "leave well enough alone." Even if it's not really "well enough," they are reluctant to look beneath the surface and understand their insecurities. Nevertheless, you can still foster an authentic relationship with them by being yourself and providing a nurturing, encouraging environment.

I attended a networking event and spotted Jason, a powerful business mogul, surrounded by a circle of admirers, as it had just become public that he had sold his company. With his contagious laughter and twinkling eyes, he appeared to thrive amidst the sea of well-wishers. I met up with Jason at the bar, and nonchalantly, said, "Sometimes, it can be a little disconcerting to sell your business as it's part of your identity." Jason looked away from the bartender and directly at me. He nodded his head, and gave me a knowing smile. This was enough. This was as far as Jason was going at this point. He knew that I knew there were some unsettling feelings underneath the celebratory umbrellas. Over time, and with my continued encouragement, Jason gradually opened up more about what he was going through. We slowly continued to develop a rapport and eventually a real connection.

As this example illustrates, you must be careful not to cross boundaries, either by pushing these men to reveal more than they are comfortable with—or by revealing so much as to make them uncomfortable. Just be yourself, gingerly exposing some of your little butts, and validate even minor self-revelations. In this way, you will enable them to lower their guard and eventually trust that they can be themselves with you. This is not always simple, and it does not always work even after a few tries. Men's big butts are usually very, very well protected.

A case in point is Adam. He would dislike me referring to him by his first name, as he likes using his first, middle, and last names (especially III) to indicate his impressive ancestry. I met with Adam on several occasions, encouraging him to become more involved with a nonprofit board that we both sat on. While he willingly agreed to meet, I could never get him to talk about anything other than his strengths. He spent most of his time trying to impress me with his business acumen and other personal accomplishments. If I dared attempt to share any type of vulnerability, he would retreat into his self-protective shell and end the meeting. The only big butts he would consider sharing were those of other board members. At my wits end, I tried my most gentle cajoling, "Is there any role or committee that you would be uncomfortable with?"

Sitting up straight, he gruffly replied, "No, I'd be good in any role I wished to take on. I just am not interested in becoming any more involved." It was time to back off. I would simply allow him to continue protecting his big butt and to keep his present role.

Ms. Perfect

We all know Ms. Perfect. She is tall, or if not, carries herself as if she were. She has a trendy, but not too trendy haircut—recently coiffed by the hottest stylist. She wears a tailored Armani suit, carries the latest Birkin, and accessorizes prudently to complement her image. She would rather walk barefoot on hot coals than admit her Manolos were hurting her feet.

She rarely looks at us, but right past us. Actually, she seems to be doing us a favor if she deems to acknowledge us at all. She is harried in a controlled manner, attending to her very important life—but, never frazzled. It is easy to be intimidated by Ms. Perfect. In her presence, if we are not careful, we can feel our own big butts growing wider; our cellulite rapidly reproducing right under her judgmental gaze. We can't stand her.

The good news is that we are not alone. Nobody likes Ms. Perfect. No one really wants her to succeed. While, to her face, we may pay homage to this goddess; behind her back—we begrudge her very existence. We resent that her superiority feeds into our own feelings of inferiority. We detest that she seems to forbid genuine communication.

The other good news is that, as we discussed in the chapter on how we cover up our big butts, believe it or not, Ms. Perfect has her own big butt. Even though she is loath to acknowledge or, heaven forbid, expose it—it does exist. Oftentimes, it is simply her need to maintain this facade of perfection, or it may be her paralyzing fear that we may spot her shortcomings.

It is certainly challenging enough to simply deal with Ms. Perfect let alone attempt to make a real connection with her. Trust me though; Ms. Perfect's shell can be cracked. You will need to apply the same principles as you used in making connections with men. Maintain your own authenticity, create a hospitable, safe environment, and give it time.

Priscilla was my Ms. Perfect. We were involved with the same organization. I sat through many meetings, victim of her all-knowing, yet distrusting glare. She particularly disliked me because I refused to abide by her rules. She withheld all emotion and showed no affect. She loved portraying herself as mysterious and hard to read. While she escalated her efforts to perfect her facade, I maintained my flawed, but genuine, persona. I showed passion when I was excited by ideas, and didn't hesitate to laugh out loud, if appropriate. I dressed professionally, but not perfectly. I even attended one meeting with DIY patchwork to a chipped nail! Her disdain progressed to hatred when I was chosen, in her mind, over her, for a highly visible position.

In being appointed to this position, I learned an invaluable lesson. Whether we admit it out loud or not, we expect Ms. Perfect to excel. When she does, we yawn. However, when we mortals excel—we inspire. Others look at our achievements and recognize that we refuse to let anything, not any of our big butts, sabotage our success. They become our cheerleaders and will do whatever they can to help us advance our accomplishments.

For me, my "victory" was shallow. I was not finished with Priscilla. True victory would be achieved only by breaking through her lines of defense and forming a real relationship. So, I arranged to sit next to her at the following meeting. Here, where she was hostage to my presence, I looked her directly in the eyes and asked her out to lunch. She accepted.

Now, over Cobb salads, came the ultimate test—I proceeded with caution. I began by genuinely validating the positive contributions she had made to our organization, sending the message that I recognized her strengths. "Priscilla, I want you to know that I admire your wisdom and determination. I don't know of anyone else who could have convinced our board to spend the money to hire a consultant, yet you did it. And, you were right. Their findings saved us an enormous amount of money." Then, I demonstrated that I was not afraid to show her my weaknesses. I tested the waters by sharing some of my concerns regarding my future responsibilities. "I really give you credit, with your determination goes patience and perseverance. I am so impatient. I hope my restlessness and impatience won't cause me problems down the road dealing with an entity that is so slow to respond."

I proceeded to ask her carefully crafted questions, looking for an opportunity to induce her to lower some of her guard. Finally, I hit the jackpot. "Isn't your youngest daughter applying for college next year?" I delved. Bingo!

Her body language visibly readjusted. Those perfectly upright shoulders slumped. Her eyes lowered. Her voice softened. "Yes."

Holding my breath I tiptoed into even deeper waters. Softly, I shared, "I still feel the pain of my children leaving home. I spent the months before their departure crying over old home movies and baby pictures. I couldn't believe it was over. It wasn't just that they were leaving—but, more that I felt like my role as a mother was ending. I felt such a loss of purpose."

She looked at me. Perhaps for the very first time—she really looked at me. "I hate it! I don't know what I am going to do," she finally allowed herself to confess.

I treasured her honesty and felt new stirrings of compassion. I did not minimize her feelings but went on to encourage her by sharing some more of my own journey. "I can so relate! I need to tell you that, my role as a mother has remained intact. I am their mother and will always be their mother. We've all survived—and our relationships have thrived."

Priscilla and I, though we never became best friends, at least now have a more genuine relationship of mutual respect. I admire her for all that she has accomplished and I have connected with her over one of our mutual big butts. As with every big butt sharing session, I kept her vulnerabilities in strict confidence. We can trust each other.

Whether we are dealing with a Ms. Perfect, a man, or anyone else reluctant to share, it is important for us to use our skills to provide an environment conducive to sharing. The skills are the same ones we use for everyone else; we just need to apply them with a little more patience and persistence. Some people like Priscilla and the litigator, will surprise you and willingly reveal their big butts. Others, while not coming clean, will at least be more relaxed and open. Wherever they fall on this spectrum, go slowly and gauge their reactions. Be vigilant in determining how far to go—stop if you perceive them becoming too uncomfortable. The following guidelines will help you share your big butt and have others reciprocate in these difficult relationships:

1. **DON'T PLAY THEIR GAME**—By refusing to put on a facade of perfection, you are negating the rules of their game. Showing you are comfortable with your own big butt sets the stage for sharing. Retain your authenticity while at the same time being extremely mindful of only sharing what is appropriate. You want to avoid making anyone feel threatened.

2. **GO SLOWLY AND GENTLY**—When people wear extra layers of protection to hide their flaws, they will not

easily disrobe. Take your time and go slowly. Help them to test the waters and discover that the world will not come to an end if they show a tiny bit of butt. This will make them feel safer and they may eventually be willing to peel off additional protective layers.

3. **PROVIDE A SAFE ENVIRONMENT**—Those who are most protective of their big butts often have the least tolerance for criticism and are the most appreciative of validation. Use this knowledge and look for appropriate opportunities for genuine reinforcement. Try to avoid criticizing or putting them in a defensive position.

4. **MAINTAIN THE HIGHEST LEVEL OF CONFIDENTIALITY**—Never disclose *anything* that they confide to you. I want to underscore this, as sometimes we repeat things that *we* consider benign. People who do not want to share—do not want even seemingly innocuous information repeated. They tend to interpret any evidence that you have revealed their disclosures as traitorous. Keep your mouth shut.

5. **SHOW CONFIDENCE AND COMPETENCE**—Do NOT regress to a needy or flirty role. You want to be your genuine and strong self. You want to show confidence and competence. You want people to open up to you because they respect you and conclude that you are someone they would like to share with. You are strong—but accepting.

6. **USE APPROPRIATE ICEBREAKERS**—In trying to share with those who are uncomfortable sharing, you must carefully tiptoe through the minefields. Use benign icebreakers as you try to uncover firm grounds.

7. **LISTEN AND OBSERVE**—Really listen to what these people are saying and not saying. Carefully observe their body language. By sharpening your observational skills you will pick up on appropriate cues either encouraging you to proceed or, clearly saying enough.

Sometimes, the most rewarding relationships are formed by reaching out to those who do not easily connect with others. Your relationship can be especially meaningful to those who are accustomed to superficial interactions. However, some people simply cannot relate in a genuine matter. All you can do is proficiently throw them a rope. If they refuse to grab on—this says something about them, not about you. Do not take this personally, simply move on.

Chapter Ten

GET OFF YOUR BUTT!

WE CAN NEVER RECLAIM THE MOMENTS, HOURS, WEEKS, AND years we've lost wishing that we were something that we were simply never going to be. We could not sell, trade, recycle, or dispose of those parts of ourselves that we deemed disgraceful—our big butts. So, instead we personified them—we gave them life. We allowed them to rule and define us. We became their subjects; succumbed to their control. Bowing to their boundaries, we abandoned our dreams and squelched our ambitions. We kept ourselves from applying to the best schools and for the best jobs. We even married the wrong men—under the illusion that they were the only ones who would have us. We held ourselves back from being what we could be and doing what we could do. Sometimes we even gave up hope.

What's done is done. But now, it's our time. We have taken back the reins of our lives. We have learned that we are the ones who anointed our big butts to power. No longer—we have reclaimed control. We've learned that we do not have to love our flaws—but we do have to accept them.

We must make up for lost time. We deserve to write the script for the rest of our lives. We can reach as high as we allow ourselves to stretch—there are no longer limitations.

If we seek to put our efforts into furthering our career—we need to identify and promote our professional persona. It is our choice. And we can pursue this choice without the weight of hiding or overcompensating for *anything* about ourselves.

The easiest way to get to where we are headed is with the help and direction of others. Therefore, we need to form relationships with those who know the way and with those who will buy our products, champion our causes, and contribute to our interests. The biggest lesson we have learned is that we can form these precious relationships just by being ourselves and allowing others to be themselves. No more artificial facades.

And if we do not want to do it for ourselves—we should do it for our daughters, our actual daughters, or those women who come after us. How dare we allow another generation of women to follow our bad examples, to define themselves by things that do not matter? How dare we allow another generation to limit their reach because of inconsequential imperfections? We must begin today and give our daughters the message that they are enough—they must not carry around the superficial expectations that have weighted down our own lives.

And if you do not want to do it for yourself or your daughters—do if for women. We have strived so hard to break through barriers—some even thicker than any put up by our big butts. More of us need to break through. While we can't remove all the outside blockades—we can at least remove the ones that we have personally constructed. It's our turn. It's our time. Get off your butt.

READING GROUP DISCUSSION QUESTIONS

1. Laura writes, "Everybody has a big butt." Do you agree? Why or why not?

2. Have you identified your own big butt? Are you comfortable sharing it with the group? Why or why not?

3. In Chapter Three Laura describes seven ways in which we deal with our big butts: (1) The Needy, (2) The Non Promoter, (3) The Tyrant, (4) The Avoider, (5) The Perfectionist, (6) The Egotist, and (7) The Pleaser. Do you see yourself in any of these categories? Which ones? Do you know people who fit these categories? Have you ever considered that they were hiding their big butts?

4. Do you agree that it is hard to quit blaming our big butts for what we dislike about ourselves? Why or why not?

5. Name the five women that you most admire. Why do you admire them? Would any of them grace the cover of a fashion magazine?

6. Do you think society has strict rules that demand perfection? Are these rules changing?

7. Do you purposefully and intentionally promote your nonprofit or business interests? Why or why not? Ask the other members for ideas on how to promote your work and share your own ideas for promoting their work.

8. When was the last time you shared your imperfections with someone else? How did they react? How did you feel? If not, what stops you from revealing?

9. When was the last time someone shared their imperfections with you? How did you feel? How did you react?

10. Can you think of one person with whom you would really like to pursue a relationship but you sense a resistance? Discuss ways in which you can break through this resistance.

11. What is the difference between a big butt and a big but?

12. Do you think that men and women deal with their big butts differently? If so, how?

ACKNOWLEDGMENTS

I AM DEEPLY GRATEFUL TO MY FAMILY AND FRIENDS FOR THEIR unwavering support, advice, and encouragement. A special thank-you goes to Gail and Susan, who patiently obsessed with me over this manuscript. I also want to thank Lauren, Suzy, Mark, David, Debbie, Robin, my editor, Anne Dubuisson Anderson, who believed in this book from the very beginning, my copyeditor, Barbara Crawford, and my designer, Daniel Kohan, Sensical Design & Communication.